BORUT LESJAK

SOUL SYNTAX

STUDIO ✦ BLEST

SOUL SYNTAX
Outcreating the Mind
by Awakening Awareness

By Borut Lesjak

SOUL AWARENESS AWAKENING
series, book 1

www.borutlesjak.com

SOUL
SYNTAX

FOR SPIRIT

Contents

SOUL
SYNTAX

Hello and Welcome

My name is Borut Lesjak and this humble book is an honest invitation to your own presence in our incredible life.

I'd like to chat about what I believe is the most important thing in the world: *awareness*.

What is awareness? I don't know. And I believe nobody knows. Moreover, what we're being taught in schools, by our parents, and later on from various sources, spiritual or mundane, is incomplete—if not downright misleading.

They say awareness *is* the mind, or is *in* the mind, or is *of* the mind. Or they say it is *not* the mind, but it comes to the same—because what they say is said *from* the mind *to* the mind.

To talk about awareness, we need to use a new syntax that is not even a syntax at all. I'll return to this, of course, from many angles and vibes. We have to build it together, you and I, as we go. It must be fresh, not pre-programmed in the slightest.

It *is* vital: as humans, we need to learn about what awareness truly is if we want to survive as a race on this enchanted, glorious planet.

But how?

Well, you see, it's not about what I have to say to you or what you wish to hear or learn. It never was. To me, this life is not a school class, nor is it a proving ground. I only say that to stress that we probably don't know what life is and may never know. Can we leave it at that and enjoy the mystery?

The main reason I am writing this book, or should I say, what gives me the faith and determination to do it, is the tiny subtle difference in the way I believe this work is being created, right now, as I'm typing this very sentence: "I feel you"—because I do feel you.

I do feel you leaning in and exchanging with this!

Whether you are sitting there in your room, or lying in your bed before going to sleep, or sunbathing on the beach, I sense you and I can connect to your focus and curiosity as you open up to receive my message in a time-bottle.

This book is *alive* in the sense that it will be different each time you read it.

And let me emphasize this now: *you matter*! You matter to me as the co-creator of this book, and also as a fellow human being, but also to everyone and everything else: you matter. We all do, but you matter in your own specific, unique way. It's up to you if you ever want to explore your uniqueness and become aware of it. But no matter what anybody says, you do matter. That's what I'm working with here. You're not merely one of my anonymous readers, just a number or a name.

You are you and this I write for you.

Now it's up to you to pause and take this in.

Are you aware that it is merely your choice whether you believe it or not?

... (pause)

This book has the power to transform your life, simply because you are reading it and are willing to do the work. You are the one shifting something in your life. The reason I am bringing this up right here at the beginning is because it's probably the most important aspect of what I wish to convey: if you're willing to *honestly engage* with what we're discussing, you will allow yourself to open a new gate into the unknown and expand your consciousness in an unprecedented way.

Yes, it is possible. But you need to play along. How would it feel to snap out of our lifelong distrust and cynicism and ignite our childlike wonderment once more?

I promise to do my best and keep pushing us—but only gently—on our common journey through the labyrinths of prior knowledge, expectations, and resistance, you and me both. In fact, I might be the one needing your support every now and then. So please trust me as much as you can trust yourself and let's go: here's my hand!

I've had some highly unusual, extraordinary experiences in my life that I'll share with you. Each of these events is almost indescribable because of how I felt inside—I perceived and sensed myself and the world in ways so different from what we are used to that it's difficult to find proper words.

These experiences shaped my personal viewpoints uniquely, and even though I've read many books about awareness, I still feel confident that I have something of my own to contribute that might actually change our lives, at least a little bit.

I've lived through many decades of being torn apart, time and again, by the innermost desire to put these fine threads of my experience together and wrap them around my mind—without thinking I'll ever be able to fully understand the whole picture.

As I write this, I feel that I'm not coming from any place of authority other than a vulnerable willingness to risk everything by trusting my intuition and showing up, against all odds. I need no other kind of confidence in order to trust myself, and to trust *you* too.

Do *you* trust yourself?

Are you ready to let go and open up? What if there *is* more to life—and you are about to finally unlock that now? Perhaps even more importantly: our common work here—as we do it together—might create another dent in the whole human collective belief system.

I have a dream that one day awareness will be the central subject—and object—presented in schools, instead of the mind and everything pertaining to the mind only. We won't just be speaking *about* awareness, but *from* and *with* awareness!

Why do I believe this is so important? Because in those strange states that I experienced, I witnessed exactly how the human being is *trapped in the mind* and how that causes all our suffering in the world. I also saw that the most important action we can undertake to break free is to *suspend our linear thinking*.

If you want to hear more, let me explain in the following chapters what I mean by that. I'll talk primarily about the difference between our awareness and our thoughts in the mind. The way I experience it, being aware is the foundation of everything *real* in our lives.

So our only way out lies in letting our awareness in.

Yes. We need to learn what awareness is, but not as the mind would ever define it. We need to *become all awareness* and witness it firsthand. At the same time, we'll begin to know ourselves.

For the gentle purposes of this book, I will be carefully proposing certain definitions and imbuing words with fresh meanings. For example, I will work with the word *miscreation* and the three terms *submind*, *undermind*, and *overmind*—which in essence stand for the same notion. I wish to make our understanding fluid, with the mind at ease, almost detached or asleep, yet *we* will still know what we're talking about.

Many luminous persons whom I respect and love, have coined and defined some of the terms I use—or *don't* use—or even use in a completely different way. I have my creative reasons for this: I believe that at this particular stage of exploring and playing around with *soul syntax*, definitions that are too correct, clear, and exact may be more of a hindrance than assistance. However, if you are inclined to study those other sources and translate my words to yours, feel free to do that by all means—that is your sovereign choice to make. We are all doing that anyway, whether we are aware of it or not.

The true value of this book is not its information, but hopefully its soul: the vibe coming from the Spirit through our *exchanging* with it. You see, it is not possible to talk about awareness using the mind alone. We may believe it is and we definitely keep trying, but we're only ever going in circles, sinking even deeper into the quicksand of our made-up reality. You too can directly witness this by yourself when your awareness grows within and you learn to trust its voice: *intuition*.

We'll talk about that more as we go.

So are you willing to accompany me into this rabbit hole, and at least for a little while, drop your defenses and simply pretend you know nothing about awareness—and the mind, for that matter? The ultimate trap, mind you, is nothing more than that: sticking to your beliefs in the mind without willingness to expand beyond what you know, and to risk it all for something so vague and untouchable that it takes your whole being and infinite *faith* to merely try the first step. But once you're sincerely willing, the path unfolds before you as if you created it out of thin air.

Shall we take this step together?

"Awakening is absolutely inevitable."
—Ink by Star, Book 1: *Orion*

Awareness of Death

This chapter, like some others later in the book, tells a plain, true story from my life. You can subtly sense that the voice of the storyteller in these chapters is not *my* voice though. It is the voice of the internal dialog that was going on in my head at the times of the events described—and though I may not necessarily agree with it any longer, I will respect and own it.

So let me recount how one night when I was four or five, I had my first unforgettable experience related to the awakening of awareness in me.

"You are important to the Universe, not to yourself."
—Ink by Star, Book 2: *Cassiopeia*

Daddy, why do we have to die?

Lying in my bed, I was thinking about my day: what I'd done, where I'd been, who I had been playing with.

Still not even 8 pm, I wasn't at all sleepy. Going to bed early was excruciatingly boring, practically torture. I'd prefer watching TV with my parents, but they were utterly sure respecting bedtime was of utter importance for a child's health.

I was utterly sure they were wrong.

Tossing and turning irritated me. I went still and imagined I couldn't move anymore. I pretended I was paralyzed. Maybe even dead.

Death! What a scary thought. What would it be like to die? I wondered. Would I lie just like this? Would I have thoughts at all?

I did my best to imagine a state without thoughts. I floated away, but I was still present. It wasn't that bad. But there would be no more seeing, no more hearing, no more living. Just blackness all around. Or not even that—pure void. How would I perceive that? Exactly as when I was asleep with no dreams, I thought. But each morning I would wake up again and remember I had been asleep. In death, I would never again wake up and never again would I be aware of losing consciousness for a period of time.

What does that mean, *never* again?

NEVER AGAIN! It struck me with all the meaning in the world. I felt it viscerally, bodily, emotionally, fatefully, larger than life, bigger than anything else I had ever pondered. The absolute entirety of my world shrunk into a grain of unimportance, compared to this. The certainty of how monumental a game-changer it was left me no doubts. Even though I was just a small boy, I understood it perfectly.

I understood death. Intuitively and instinctively, I knew exactly what dying entailed. I knew what *forever* meant.

An unprecedented clarity filled me.

I was *awake*, aware of the larger picture, the totality of life, and death.

And death... it was completely inevitable! Nothing could stop me from dying, absolutely nothing! Whatever happened and no matter when it occurred, there would come a moment of the naked truth: the point of dying! There was no escaping that! Nowhere to hide! Nothing to be done!

Death was coming!

A total shock overtook me, gripping me with unspeakable truth, like a wailing alarm clock you couldn't snooze. My tiny body was filled with adrenaline and like a spring I was propelled up and out of my bed!

I didn't know why, but I had to do something physical about it. My heart pounded in my chest, wanting to explode. The sensation was untenable. I was being urged to emerge into life again.

I dashed into the living room with tears streaming and leapt into my dad's embrace. He instantly understood something strange was going on. He didn't send me back to bed but got ready to listen instead.

"Dad..." I squeezed out words in between sobs. "Why do we have to die?"

He sat straight. He looked at me calmly to console me. He was visibly relaxed. I think he both realized the subject was serious, but that nothing was really wrong.

"Well, everybody and everything dies," he started to explain. "That's the nature of life." He paused to peer at me.

I wasn't convinced.

"The bees and the trees also die and everything in nature does too. So do we. Now we're alive and after we've lived a good life, we die. There's nothing wrong with that. It's how it's supposed to be."

I listened to his words, but mostly I felt his warm body against mine. I trusted his confidence. I wanted to believe he was right so much that I didn't question anything he was saying. I didn't want to go there at all—I had no need to come to the bottom of the issue. Instead, the sense of safety and security, no matter how lasting or how real, was all that I cared to experience.

"Alright," I said with a sigh, and I swept my tears away. From the corner of my eye, I noticed what was on the TV. My dad caught that and knew I was back to normal.

"Very well," he said, "Now go back to bed. You need to get some good-night sleep."

His voice became stern and commanding again, and this return to his usual self imbued me with the comforting sense that everything was as it should be. My reality was restored.

That experience marked me for life. A gateway to hell had opened. Knowing that there was something so terminal and unavoidable, and so phantasmagorically fateful awaiting me at all times, constantly, perennially, desperately, hanging above my head like the sword of Damocles...

For many years afterwards, I proceeded to deliberately avoid thinking about dying so I could feel a fake sense of safety and security instead of experiencing the nagging doubts and the indescribable, primal fear.

But wait—wasn't that jolt I experienced in my story an alarm signal, awakening me from my slumber of diminished awareness? Didn't I feel more alive and vibrant afterwards? Why would I be running away from that?

Was that awareness, or something else, awakening within me?

Well, let's not jump ahead, but go slowly instead. Baby steps.

Suffice it to point out that we all know fear very well in this life, and we also know anger and sadness. We know sorrow and grief and heartbreak, disappointment, frustration, unrequited love, feelings of unworthiness or not belonging, we know hunger and violence and sickness, we know suffering—and we know denial, our coping mechanism for any of the above.

To feel truly alive—do we have to suffer? Do we have to feel at all? How can we be happy and feel joy, but never really suffer?

How does all that work together in practice, and how does it relate to awareness, or to our soul or the Spirit?

If we awaken, what are we awakening to? Do we want to? Do we have to?

Oh, again with all these questions! Who is really asking them?

Anyway, I just want to know whether life is safe at all... How about you?

Are we destined to toil and suffer, only to die in the end?

Or is there an alternative?

A way out?

"Believe in what you really want to believe in."
—Ink by Star, Book 4: *Cygnus*

BABY STEPS

There *is* a way through this pain!

You carry the power within you, not just to learn of this way, but to *generate* it for yourself, starting right now: a way, leading you through and through, to a clear, soul-based view of the world and to an inner state of a neutral and unlimited love from where we can all end the suffering, heal, and re-create our lives, together.

There exists no secret key to unlocking some grand solution, *but* if you can in this very moment *choose* to *feel* conscious enough to glimpse through the veil of illusion, in your own terms, you will see for yourself how it is all connected and how our reality is kept in place.

That truth is yours alone.

I call it *consciousness*.

Can you *experience* it?

I mean, right now.

...

Yes, it starts with a choice: a willingness to *do* something.

Remember how I talked about us both co-creating this mysterious path in front of us and how it's entirely up to you whether you engage or not? So whenever I invite you to do something actively instead of merely reading it in the mind, it's your chance, your choice, and your call about what you're going to do about it.

The next step is to intentionally place your complete focus on something, anything, thus pausing the mind so you can become aware of yourself and the world around you.

Anything can serve as your new point of focus: you may look around and observe something that catches your attention briefly, or close your eyes and draw a breath, or, with your buttocks and thighs, simply feel the chair you're sitting on. Smile.

This conscious action will distract the mind momentarily, and that's what we want. I call it a distraction, but it could also be referred to as *grounding*.

Now you are in the present moment, where your power lies, as they say. Add some humor to it, as I just did, because seriousness is the forte of the mind. I promise I'll tell you later why we are trying to slightly circumvent the mind—please, just trust me on this one for now.

Sooner or later, you may feel that you are inadvertently and barely perceptibly slipping back into a familiar daily stupor with all the background noise in the mind that offers you a false sense of safety. Well, just re-focus once again! That's the trick. It can become our practice. Yes, we *train* our awareness. We train at awakening. We'll come back to this.

When I find myself losing my awareness, I take a deep, conscious breath. I'll take one right now, as I write this.

...

Ah, it feels so good! I am alive, again.

At this point, as throughout this book, I will invite you to please join me drawing such loving breaths. Do it your way, by all means, but do it. Therein lies the difference between just talking about the path and actually walking it. This can be your call.

In the present moment, you can focus on a grain of sand, so to speak, in a laser-like manner, and forget everything else. Or, you can expand to include all the rest of your life without ever leaving the present, staying right here and now, but also sensing and intuiting all that you are, have been, and are becoming. You can inspire yourself to glance at the larger picture of the world, centered still in your current moment, *this* moment.

Consider the following questions, if you will—this is something that you can actively engage with: pause within, take a breath, maybe even close your eyes and feel your body.

...

Remember you're alive, you matter, and you love yourself.
Now imagine this: how will you die?
Who were you before you were born?
What hue is your impact on your fellow beings?
What do you want it to be?
Again, are you still *here*? Don't even think about thinking. That was a joke, not a command, of course. Just some of my humor. Let's be gentle with ourselves.

Floating like a wisp of fog, stretching from here to eternity, being aware of all that is at once, while the age-old restrictions, certainties, and top-priority missions of your life are cracking open, peeling and falling off like broken, rusty armor. No more suffocating your true power, the power of awakened awareness!

A series of incredible experiences I had throughout my life led me to gradually accept a brand new and intrinsically original view of the world. From where I stand, the only true dimension in this Universe is the one of awareness. Each of us, at any given moment, is more or less awakened, or open, to awareness.

You can call it awareness, or Spirit, or God, or anything else: it doesn't matter what you call it—it only counts when you actually experience its flow through your very being, such as a vibration or a current in the physical body. And even that is only the first step.

When you let Spirit enter your energy field and you focus your attention on its flow through you, and if the mind relaxes enough to relinquish its otherwise constant control, you will awaken to something indescribable: consciousness!

Some call that enlightenment. To me, it's more like just a shard, only one piece of the whole that has yet to come together. So I call it a *quantum enlightenment* (but not overly seriously) and I believe that we have to make it our responsibility, a sacred duty, to re-awaken daily and gather all the quantum enlightenments at our disposal, thus doing our individual part of something which is of cosmic importance: helping bear Spirit completely into this Universe.

On a personal level, consciousness is the only thing that is real in this life.

All else is a contorted, unchecked fabrication, twisted by our pre-programmed perception and cognition, and molded by our fears, expectations, and beliefs.

All else—is a dream.

And in a dream, you can awaken without waking up from the dream.

You can become aware of your dreaming and of the true reality of your dream.

You can become conscious.

My intention here is to reach beyond the present limitations of what we believe we know about the mind, the spirit, and awareness, and offer you this book as yet another original approach to self-awakening. We may indeed need many...

Even as a small child, I would have the most profound experiences of *remembering* that there is more to life than we can usually perceive and believe. Years later, during a noisy recess in high school when I was fifteen, something awakened in me. Something shifted in me.

I emerged as if through a veil of fog and peeked, from behind the wraps of the mind, at a whole different world, a greater scheme of things outside of my customary, ever-present fears, convictions, and views—outside my old story.

That singular experience was self-fulfilling and needed no external explanation or support. It changed my life's trajectory for good. Later on, I had many other similar experiences that added to my awakening in a cumulative way.

Through the samples of my personal experiences, which are all I truly have and know, I'll pave an alternative viewpoint of the workings of the mind. I will open us up to the possibility that we may all indeed be somehow trapped in a super mysterious and vicious circle here in this world. Yet in the same breath I'll endeavor to untangle the sticky mess of our confusion, resistance, and denial, so the crystal clear light of your own soul's consciousness can shine brightly through the whole wider vista and help you release the seeming control of the mind's grip.

If these words don't hold any meaning for you, that's fine too. The sense lies beneath, and within. You can feel it in your beating heart.

The essence of what I'm proposing is simple: take this matter into your own hands, now!

Do you want to get clear, heal your life, and maybe help others with that as well?

All you need to do is take the first, next step.

The direction, at this point, is not important. As you will see for yourself, you are in the center, and all paths lead outwards, breaking free.

Are you curious?

"You don't have to go anywhere else to start your inward journey."
—Ink by Star, Book 8: *Aries*

Awareness of Life

When I was a child, I felt that everything around me was so alive and vibrant: scents smelled richer, colors were brighter, and it was all just so much more real.

Why?

"All is dance. We are music."
—Ink by Star, Book 3: *Andromeda*

A midsummer day's dream

A young boy, perhaps nine years old, with intelligent, compassionate blue-green eyes and disheveled fair hair, was sitting on the balcony in the heat of a brilliant lazy summer afternoon. A soft breeze caressed the world, making the air temperature much more enjoyable. Scents of recently mown grass and of drying hay in the nearby field mixed with the enticing smell of colorful, bee-covered flowers, creating nostalgic memories in the boy's mind. The stillness was complete, just as the blueness of the sky was immaculate. C'est la vie!

I was that boy.

From behind the house, a loud noise penetrated the peaceful rest, only adding to the aliveness of the experience. The neighbor's dog barked wildly, absorbed in his role of a home guardian, pretending the threat was more imminent than it was, as the cat nonchalantly strolled by on the dusty gravel road. Fine cement was escaping to the wind from the mixer that had been diligently making concrete, and the powerful rusty rock grinder was hungrily devouring its long-awaited meal, making frightening crunching and creaking sounds with its iron jaws, crushing hefty stones into sand. My grandfather was supervising the work, smoothly helping the flow of rocks entering the grinder, with a meditative look of satisfaction on his weathered face.

I sighed out of profound joy, playing with the sunlight on my eyelashes as they made the appearance of rainbows. I felt thirsty so I jumped up and ran into the kitchen to make some sweet homemade raspberry syrup with crystal clear tap water that I first let run till it got cold. Oh, how delightful it was! How it quenched my thirst and cooled my body. I quivered from pleasure. Washing the glass quickly, I replaced it in the cupboard. I glanced at the blue and white porcelain clock on the adobe-tiled chimney. Time passed slowly. Two hours still before lunch...

I returned to the balcony and grabbed my book. Instantly I was immersed in the fantastic story. When the drone of a passing plane captured my attention, I looked up from the page. My mind was still half in the fantasy, half in reality. Moved by the character in the story, I contemplated where I was, *who* I was. A profound emotion engulfed me. I was aware of my life, of my bliss. With a softened gaze, I intently followed the imaginary line the plane drew in that vastness of the infinite sky. I closed the book, keeping my thumb tucked in where I left off reading, and sighed in peace and contentment. If I was a cat, I'd purr.

I felt a notable shift in my awareness, not unlike when suddenly waking up from a good dream in the morning, smiling. I studied the sky and it seemed to me that the soft blue color had just become more intense—truer, somehow. It appeared to be turning to a more magical, tourmaline hue. My whole life had just become more real. I glanced at the deep green cover of my book and was surprised to see that the color was not just a color—it was strikingly vivid! Alive! Everything was illuminated with an inner shine, a magnificent glow. I leapt up and leaned on the balcony railing. I carefully swept the landscape with my gaze, circling my known universe widely and attentively. Yes, everything was the same and yet nothing was the same anymore. I had awakened from my dream!

This aliveness is what and how we experience in the presence of our awakened awareness. We can't really control it and get there on demand. It almost seems as if it just happens of its own accord, arbitrarily. But what we can do is to prepare space for it, open the door in our hearts and invite the awareness in. We can *will* it, *intend* it, and keep training our awakening daily, as often as we possibly can.

Do you want to awaken to your life?

"Awareness is not under your control and awakening not under
your command. Let go."
—Ink by Star, Book 4: *Cygnus*

WHY ARE YOU READING THIS BOOK?

Meditate daily.

That's it.

That's this whole book in two words.

If you meditate daily you likely don't need this book, so you can lay it down and instead take a walk, sit in the sun, listen to the wind or rain, play with children, have fun, or go to the office and do some work. Do anything you want. There is nothing else you need to learn in this lifetime.

But if you struggle with trying to exactly comprehend the why and how and when, read on. If you want to find your place, know your value, and sail more peacefully through life, this book will guide you safely towards *your* inner compass.

You see, this is not as much about explaining anything as it is about inspiring and instilling faith in your own power of awareness and love. Your self-love.

So what's the deal with the mind and awareness?

Knowing the true difference between the mind and awareness is key. It is the same difference as knowing, when you are dreaming, that you are dreaming. That knowing is only possible through consciousness.

It is only when you awaken from dreaming that you know you were dreaming. Or do you?

Beware, I might be playing around as the devil's advocate, saying the opposite of what I believe here. Remember: for you, it only matters what *you* believe.

The whole point *I* want to make in this book is a discernment between thinking and being conscious. You see, when you are dreaming a normal dream and then wake up to your real life—the way I see it, you didn't really awaken at all, you merely changed dreams. To awaken means for your consciousness to arise and significantly heighten and illuminate your cognitive processes. I'm not talking merely about shifting to a higher gear. I'm talking about a full quantum leap to a whole new game!

I'm talking about awakening *within* a dream, not from a dream. One moment you're totally immersed in the reality and values of your dream, identifying with the character or role you are enacting, and the next moment—swoosh!—a deep wind of Awareness lifts the fog off of your perception and awareness of the world around you, and also within.

You become conscious of everything at once, as if for the first time ever, but simultaneously you know fully well that you've been there and that before, countless times.

Still, soon after, the mist will creep back onto you, clouding your consciousness but suggesting you are still completely awake, and you will get lost again, for who knows how long, until the wind of Awareness blows again.

And again.

And again...

We would need a new syntax to be able to talk and even think about the mind and awareness without missing the point! What *is* the point? We'll circle back to that before the end of the book. We need to lay and ground some foundations first.

For reasons I never understood, I've been guided and driven to pay close attention to anything pertaining to the mind/awareness duality around me, and within. At certain times in my life, this was the only subject under the sun I found truly interesting and important.

I have read my fair share of words that countless wise beings have put forward, but none of that ever completely expressed what I myself intuited and experienced daily in my own unique way. There are certainly clear connections and common denominators among the knowledge at large about this subject, but I believe many more fresh approaches should be taken and brought forth at this time in our history. And I *know* I'm far from being alone in this viewpoint.

This book is my honest attempt at one such novel approach.

Now, as much as I'd like to, I can't skip ahead to tell you the gist of it, and not because it is too hard or convoluted—but because it is *circular*. It is in fact super simple—just not to the mind. So we need to build a whole other avenue of *pure understanding* first—a new syntax!

During the length of this short book, the notions and meanings will weave a canopy of support, but the true value will emerge energetically from between the lines.

Call it an invitation to sincere introspection that might well lead to the first in a series of your quantum enlightenments, as I call them, only half in jest.

Consider this: perhaps you will be able to *smell* or *taste*—more than understand—the real difference between the mind and awareness. As we juxtapose the two, a parallax view will shine, creating new perceptions about the very fabric of creation.

I will endeavor to share my deepest transcendental experiences and fateful personal events with you as a canvas on which we'll work, not by adding, but by subtracting: erasing, clearing, opening up our viewpoints and beliefs, then distilling a solution out of our inner creation.

Nevertheless, ultimately only you can teach yourself about what awareness is and mind isn't. You will need to hear the call to assuming your own responsibility, and trusting yourself in the process.

I strongly suggest you take charge, proactively.

Nobody can bestow this power onto you, it has to be claimed and generated within.

Do you *feel* what I mean?

Just imagine that you really need no further information on this.

To know awareness is to experience it within, and the avenue to arriving there lies outside of any kind of knowledge we may ever obtain or possess. Now simply take a deep breath again, and practice your awakening. Let it come from your heart—and please believe me that it is still good if you just *make it up*, for now!

...

You are ready: you are reading this.

"Being aware that you are dreaming does not make you awake."
—Ink by Star, Book 8: *Aries*

FIRST ENLIGHTENMENT

Awake

There was so much noise!

It was recess. The classroom was a crazy mess. My school mates were laughing, yelling, running around and between the desks, knocking chairs over, and sweeping pencils and wooden triangles onto the floor in complete disdain.

They were just having fun, unwinding, using every second of those fifteen available minutes to temporarily forget about the problems and fears constantly lurking beneath the fabric of our existence. But for once I couldn't relax. I couldn't unwind. I felt it.

Silent pressure.

Underneath us.

Everywhere.

It was the darkness of expectations that just wouldn't go away. The underlying fear that teenagers had, including the terror of being called upon in class to answer but then being examined and found guilty and worthless, the constant urgency to be good, to do enough. The demands of others upon us.

I felt strange.

Sitting at my desk, as my classmates played around me, I witnessed my vision turning peripheral. I defocused completely. I heard the ruckus, muffled now, as if it was coming from someplace far away—maybe from another dimension altogether.

Something happened.

I was realizing something.

I became acutely aware of two things: of my life as it was, the boxed-in reality I lived in, and at the same time I realized how much more there was to life! I was here, present within the flow of everyday energies, my classmates jumping around me, my body sitting quietly at my desk, but at the same time I was removed, distanced, untouchable.

I was eternal, even now.

I was infinite, even being finite.

I was awake!

So awake, in fact, that my normal life seemed like a dream. All our endeavors, our expectations, our efforts, our anxieties—they were not real. All our sweat and blood, all fake. Futile.

It just didn't matter.

Nothing did. The grades, the success, not even the education and knowledge itself. Not really. Not ultimately and eternally...

I felt a swell of love and I knew.

Only our love was true.

I could see this clearly. We were souls, coming to this planet to love, arriving to where we were, even right inside this school and this classroom. My classmates were shouting and I was not—but we were all here to love.

Everything else suddenly seemed beside the point.

I felt a powerful, undying love for everyone here, for my friends, for the teachers—for all souls, equally. I wished I could tell them what I felt. I wanted to save them from their demons, fears, obsessions.

I stared at them and realized they had no idea what I was feeling. I was feeling it alone. I couldn't save them. I couldn't even tell them what I was feeling. I couldn't explain it to anyone.

I felt alone. I felt different. I felt separated.

I felt myself becoming lost in this bad feeling again. In this dream.

Was I drowning?

Was I drowning deep in a dream?

No.

Because I was still awake.

It was an awakening that would partially stay with me for the rest of my life.

And—I had hope now.

Big, shiny hope!

I could help myself, and then others as well.

In time.

"Everyone is asleep and I don't know how to wake them up."
—Ink by Star, Book 21: *Pegasus*

Primal Exploration

Books and scientific articles trying to explain the workings of the mind abound. I only mention them because I want to invite you to take a leap of faith together with me. You as the reader and I as the writer: let's both commit to becoming *primal explorers* for the time we need to complete this book, at the very least.

When I say a primal explorer, I mean that I feel and believe that all human beings are more than capable of studying the world around us in our own original, unique capacity, if we only allow ourselves that risky privilege. The self-confidence we require for this feat may still lie dormant in our hearts. It starts with a choice: a childlike curiosity and eagerness to undertake a path never walked before, for many of us.

If we want to explore the slippery terrain of the mind and awareness, it's of key importance to open up to the twilight of brave maybes and profound hmms, to honestly forget all that we think we already know on the subject. And I call upon you now: let's pause a little, take a juicy breath, blink twice, and dive deep within our endless ocean of being, wearing solely a naked inner perception as we proceed.

...

Now, as we steadily ask ourselves the following questions, let's be the observers of our cognitive processes.

It's crucial here, mind you, to take the time, and perhaps spend at least a minute on each of these inquiries:

Who am I? What am I doing here?
What is the mind? What is a thought?
What is life? What is death?
What is the Universe? What is God? What is a soul?
What is consciousness? What is awareness?

...

Of course, if you cheated a little bit and quickly rushed through—perhaps similar to the way you tend to briskly settle matters in your everyday life—that's perfectly alright. Don't worry about it. We all do what we can. Give yourself a bear hug and continue reading—or feel free to return to the questions above. The choice is always yours; that's where your power lies.

Now, entertain this novel notion for a moment: we are *not* looking for answers here. Instead, we are solely paying close attention to what is actually going on within us as we touch upon the questions and ponder them, without trying to be right, correct, or final in our answers.

Instead of arriving at certainty, maybe we can just say, "I don't know." Or we can intuit there are no definitive, monolithic answers—perhaps this knowing flows like a river, flickers like candlelight, or shifts like a shadow, unsubstantial, ephemeral, ghostlike.

In our society, we've been constantly geared towards succeeding. To me, exquisite liberty permeates the mood of not desiring the closure of truth. To allow ourselves to be confused, yet firmly in faith. As the inner fog starts to clear, we'll recognize that confusion belongs only to the mind, while the unknown is the realm of adventure, exploration, and joy: life!

Do you feel the freedom of being able to just pause—everything in your life—whenever you choose? A great practice for me is to simply sit down and be. I have no agenda. I don't have to accomplish anything at all. I don't need to observe and witness life as it unfolds around me, I don't have to dive deeper within and feel anything special. As I let go of my expectations and surrender myself fully to the present moment, something shifts in me and my awareness expands without any control or volition on my part. And that's when I become a true primal explorer!

Throughout this book, and maybe even in our own daily life, whenever we get a chance and feel the intuitive call to become a primal explorer, let's open up to the sensation of that no-agenda-all-is-perfect freedom again, and explore away!

We can certainly return to the exercise above as many times as needed, until we can awaken into the presence of abandon, of acquiescence to something larger than us. We may realize on some level that in life—when we are *not* primal explorers—our questions and answers are merely a game of the mind we've been playing for far too long to remain interested. We've evolved out of it now.

So what is beyond?

"Good answers are not as essential as good questions."
—Ink by Star, Book 3: *Andromeda*

Stopping the World

When I was thirty-five, something happened to me and it was by levels of magnitude the single most extraordinary experience beyond anything else in my life, except perhaps my birth, which I don't remember, or death, which I can only presume. It was indescribable in the full meaning of the word—yet here I am, describing it.

"Nothing is just an illusion and nothing is just as it seems."
—Ink by Star, Book 13: *Virgo*

The day the world stood still

At that time, I had been freshly infatuated with a girl who loved sports as a professional sportswoman, and we were happy. It was summertime. I didn't have a worry under the scorching sun by the dark blue sea where we were staying with a group of friends. A deserted, concrete tennis court with cracks crisscrossing the faint orange paint and a net that had barely survived the years overlooked the gulf from high above.

We played tennis there at noon, just because. The heat on my bare back made me feel alive. The scent of the low, dry bushes circling the perimeter melted into the sounds of zooming insects, but the cicadas had hidden, awaiting the coolness of late afternoon.

My friend excelled in all sports and I was no match for her. She danced circles around me. We played several games and I lost them all. After I missed three balls in a row, she smiled from ear to ear and ventured far into the thorny bushes to retrieve them.

Waiting for her, feeling on top of the world a hundred feet above the sea, I swirled around, extending my arms and holding my racket.

My deep breath turned into a sigh of pure joy.

My gaze swept the far horizon where the cerulean blue of the sky caressed the endless mass of seawater. Rotating on my axis mundi once again, I stared directly up. My heart opened completely.

Bliss.

Was the sky still blue or was it turning a tad purplish?

I stopped...

...and the world stopped with me.

Everything was still there, but nothing was the same any more.

Something extraordinary had happened to my perception. Not just perception—my cognition.

Spellbound, I observed.

My eyes focused on object after object and I felt that I knew them all, knew their names and functions, but I couldn't really tell for sure.

There were zero thoughts in my head, no mental processes whatsoever, only the silence of a vacuum.

The movie of life unfolding around me didn't pause, neither was it muted—but something was gone in its entirety: the mind.

For years before that, I had been practicing meditation and trying to quiet the mind. I had become quite adept at it and had learned how to stop thinking almost completely for brief periods of time. Those moments had sometimes stretched to seconds and almost to minutes, and always brought me deep serenity.

This was nothing like that.

Instantly, I just forgot all that I'd known before. I didn't know where I was, what anything was, or who I was. All the rational concepts, notions, and names of things were not merely obscured or clouded—they were absolutely no more, as if they had never been.

In retrospect, I remember I had seen colors. I could say, colors as before, but they were alive and ever-changing and I couldn't recognize them as I had no a priori knowledge of anything! The objects around me shifted and morphed imperceptibly, just like in a dream, flowing into each other yet remaining separate and individual at the same time.

My inner state was one of unprecedented calm fascination, bedazzlement with no attachments, mystery with no agenda. I had no words to assign to anything, no thoughts to formulate a notion, nothing to hold on to as a foundation I could re-build my world on—not that I wanted to anyway. I didn't know what I wanted. Yet I wasn't confused or impaired in any meaningful way. I simply was. In perfection. As if this state of being was the ultimate freedom and power.

Now I realize that at that moment I had no way of even knowing who I was, because the concept of "I" didn't exist for me. I was oneness. But it went further than that: the concept of "being" didn't exist either. Nothing was, yet everything was.

I'll never forget my first thought that arrived almost at the same time as my friend returned to the court with our yellow tennis balls.

"I wonder how long this will last..." And it was over.

As if a switch had been turned, I was my old Borut again, remembering this weird experience clearly, yet once again recognizing everything as before, knowing the names of things, and eagerly waiting to play the next game with my sweetheart. She didn't even notice anything, and I didn't mention it.

What could I possibly say? What?

It took me a good fifteen years of devoted growth to ground my otherworldly experience into a frame of reference I could understand on some level. This whole process, just like the experience itself, was not something easy to explain, and it wasn't something one would expect it to be. As I said, this is all circular.

Shall we see if we can make the full turn?

"An open mind is not a state of mind but a state of awareness."
—Ink by Star, Book 14: *Libra*

WHO ARE YOU?

It's cliché to talk about knowing yourself in this age. But I feel nothing is cliché when the Spirit is moving through you. That's the primal exploration I'd like to invite you on.

Let's both start by taking another deep breath, and even if the mind gets distracted for a little while—who cares?

...

Feel the body relax. Feel that any remnants of control are palpable, like strings attached to somewhere long ago. It doesn't have to make sense at all.

A soft, warm, fuzzy feeling dances in your chest. Let it embrace your inner heart, magnetically. The flutters of a bird, joyful, proud, present, are making you smile.

This is a moment of choice.

I choose to trust love.

Do you?

My heart is open. No expectations or agendas mar my intention. I'm here for a purpose I'm still creating, and will be until the day I leave.

I ask myself: who am I?

I'm just a guy, sitting behind my desk, typing away. I have... many people and objects and objectives in my life—but that is what I have, not who I am.

You see, this is my primal exploration. I will not even consider wording my answer around the facts and dilemmas that are so commonly put forward. Instead, I'm focusing on the void beyond the thoughts, all the while allowing my sentiments and intuition to lead the way. I dare to let go.

So, who *am* I?

I don't know. This is all an endless mystery, that much feels certain.

What does it even mean "to be"? And when I say mean, I mean that in a sense before any definitions take hold, again. See—it's circular.

Is there a way out of these cycles? Yes. It is circular only to the mind. And for as long as I base my identity largely on the mind, I will question and doubt everything.

How can I reset my identity? Isn't that the same question of *who am I?*

Indeed it is. No matter. I am now consciously bringing focus to my other sides and components, outside of the mind, as much as I can.

And I define, presently: I am whatever I identify with, if I even do.

There is freedom of the free will choices I'm making that oozes through the auras all around and within me. I am this freedom: the freedom of not even caring about the answers or truths.

I love, not care.

Now, before we drift into the abstract limbo of merely mental creation—let's ground! But not as we've been raised and taught by society: by the mind. No, quite the opposite. We'll ground into the reality of existence that I'll call Nature. To profess my undying love for Her, I'll call Her: Mother Nature.

Search for something to look at, anything. Gaze at it. Feel its existence beyond your perception.

Now feel its complete independence from you.

Can you?

I can't.

Here I played the devil's advocate again.

Our *interdependence* is our co-creation, and love is the moving agent.

Take a deep breath and feel your feet, firmly planted on the floor, your thighs, ready for a restful action, your abdomen and lower back, kindly supporting the world, your shoulders, carrying the loving suffering of life. Feel any heavy emotions mix and exchange with affection for Mother Nature and humanity. In your heart, you choose love, and you trust love. Add an *inner smile*. That's enough. That's faith.

...

Now, who am I?

I'm someone else than I was a minute ago.

I'm an integral flow of viewpoints and choices.

I see there is no singular, definitive, correct answer to that question. And perhaps it's the same when defining our entire reality: we can't, there is no final explanation at all.

What if it's better to just leave the seeming mess tangled, all curled up on itself, yet vibrant and alive with hope? Or is that another cliché: oneness?

Oh, who knows... It can be anything of the above, or below.

Who are you, now?

What are you choosing to feel right now?

"What you feel is real."
—Ink by Star, Book 15: *Scorpius*

DREAMING AWAKE

> "Whatever is possible in dreams is possible in reality."
> —Ink by Star, Book 6: *Phoenix*

The fire from within

As a youngster, I was introduced to Castaneda's books by my best friend whom I hadn't seen for a year because he was in the military service. He returned a changed man.

When we met for the first time after he got back, chatting away in my car parked in front of his block of flats, he didn't say much. He spoke briefly about the extreme hardship he had to endure and told me that one book saved his life: *The Fire from Within*. He casually produced the copy he'd apparently stolen, and inserted it into my hands. His charcoal black eyes were fierce and seemed to stress his words. "You *have* to read this!"

"Whatever," I thought to myself. I just wanted to converse about other stuff, but he didn't have time for talking away. He said *bye* and left.

At home, I threw the book onto a shelf without even looking at it. I knew better.

In the months that followed, I had the opportunity to discuss deep subjects of awareness with my friend on several occasions, and I couldn't help but admire his fresh, original viewpoints—compared to those he used to have before serving in the army—on practically everything, even the most mundane things that would normally sound plain and boring. But almost everything he uttered came to me as a surprise—including, most of all, the manner by which he seemed to obtain his information: plucking it straight out of thin air.

Intrigued by my friend and now genuinely interested, I finally resigned to pick up the book that had transmuted him so profoundly within only a year.

I randomly opened it at the beginning of the chapter *The Mold of Man* and started to read. From the first word on, I was intrigued, absorbed, and pulled into another reality that I vaguely remembered from before: from my first, high-school awakening. After devouring the whole chapter in a single bite, I slammed the book closed dramatically and once again entered an exquisite experience, absolutely unique.

An otherworldly mist of violet hue danced in front of my inner eye and spread deep into my heart and whole being. A certain infinite, real magic was readjusting the world as I'd known it. A grand opening of possibility made me sway and swoon with delight.

I knew then there was more to life than what everyone believed. But even more impressive was the fact that I'd known it all along.

You may be asking yourself at this point, where am I going with this section?

Well, I felt the call to acknowledge this important turning point in my life. Let me add that for twenty years after that event I trained my awakening of awareness, following the insights and wisdom of Castaneda's books and the ancient Mexican Indian shamans he writes about.

Those shamans immersed themselves, for many generations, into a profound, firsthand exploration of awareness. Like many other mature, indigenous cultures, they managed to create ways of extricating themselves from the ubiquitous illusion and control of the mind. Their practices and discoveries of the true nature of existence were mind-boggling.

Dreaming and *stalking* are their two avenues of expansion, the tools I had actually been working with ever since I could remember. But it was only after reading about them in Castaneda's tome that I became aware of their intricacies.

The dreaming practice is simple to describe, yet impossible to ever understand. The starting exercise, on the most basic level, is to *will* yourself to find a certain object in your dreams. That object can simply be your own hands.

A couple of years after my initial exposure to this specific technique, having remained dedicated, every night just before falling asleep, to giving myself a conscious command to look for my hands, I finally did find my hands in my dreams.

I'd had lucid dreams many times before, even as a child. When having a nightmare, I used to *remember* that I was only dreaming, and that helped me dissipate my fear and—start experimenting. In one of my dreams, for example, I let an attacking dog bite my arm, knowing fully well I'd be safe, but still awaiting the imminent sensation with trepidation: *would there be pain?*

I learned to deeply relax into free-falling from a skyscraper or into a precipice without the usual terror in my gut, and sometimes I even *dream-shifted* into the pleasure of flying—without an aircraft—around and around. I could never fly completely freely—there seemed to always be a limitation present: either I couldn't go as high as I wanted, or as fast, or I simply ran out of "fuel" and had to land, quite frustrated.

Finding my hands was somewhat different. It entailed a new level of both awareness and control. Later, I learned that the control wasn't really mine—or, it wasn't the mind's control I'd been used to.

The newly created awareness was the clarity of remembering my command to find my hands, which I had issued myself prior to falling asleep. The first time this awareness appeared, I simply remembered that there was something I needed to remember. It came as a shocking moment of awakening from a dull slumber or daydreaming.

Instantly, I received an intuitive spark of knowing that I was there for a reason—and that I was somebody else and not who I had intrinsically believed I was a moment ago. Upon awakening—within my dream—I realized I had to adopt another role to play, a more fulfilling one.

The whole process was immediate and didn't leave me much time to wonder or ponder what was going on. The mind was asleep anyway. Another part of me awakened, and I clearly knew I was dreaming, but also that I should, without any ado, lift my hands to the level of my eyes so I could take a long, attentive look at them. After doing that I felt relieved and proud, jubilant even! I was aware that I had done something special, something truly mystical.

At the same time, I was cognizant of my sleeping body somewhere undefined outside my dream. I was both at once, the sleeper and the dreamer, sleeping and awake. I didn't feel or see my body, I just knew it had to be out there—my physical body, not the one in my dreams.

After resting my gaze on the palms of my hands for some indefinite time, I lost interest. There were other adventures awaiting: flying, cavorting, having fun. My determination rapidly diminished and my focus went elsewhere. And just like when falling asleep at night, my awareness trickled away completely and blended into that enormous unknown at large, and darkness closed upon me.

I continued to practice dreaming and I became intimate with both the experience of awakening and the sensation of steadily losing my consciousness, the way a candle light would slowly suffocate, dwindle, and die. Every time, I desperately fought to retain at least a vestige of what I called control over losing myself, but it invariably slipped through my yearning, dreamful fingers.

The ancient Mexican Indian shamans called that consciousness *dreaming attention*. They claimed one can train to sustain their dreaming attention for ever longer periods of time, until a time comes when one can remain *dreaming awake* constantly.

I firmly believe, after decades of practice, that dreaming and dreaming attention are inextricably connected to getting free from the incessant control of the mind. After all, it's the same awareness, the only one we have—or should I say, *are*. We just call it meditating when it's in the daytime and dreaming when the night falls.

"Life is a real dream and death is just waking up."
—Ink by Star, Book 18: *Aquarius*

WHAT ARE YOU DOING HERE?

Why is knowing yourself, or learning to know and even love yourself, so important?

We're getting to the hard part now.

I've been repeating the idea that most of our issues around understanding awareness and reality are circular. What I mean is that there are certain notions we discuss that the mind just can't believe are beyond its capacity to ever understand, and it does not give up trying, ever. One such notion is awareness itself.

The mind doesn't see that as soon as it touches upon anything outside of its linear, digital realm, it will—instead of letting go and leaving an empty space or void in our cognition—create a projection, a replica of the real thing, which to the mind will seem perfectly real.

In fact, in order to make the whole of reality appear seamless, the mind will proceed to create a veneer of projections on top of absolutely everything it can possibly think about, externally or internally, real or abstract.

The mind alone is never capable of seeing through its own deception.

So that which the mind honestly believes is awareness, is merely the surrogate of true awareness—something collapsed and simplified to a degree that the mind can work with. The mind will never know the difference between its projection and the real thing.

As primal explorers, when we go deeper and clearer into the essence of all things, we want to be aware of that. We may need to be extra gentle and patient with the mind—talking to it almost like we talk to small children or pets.

The softer I focus on feeling humanity and our world, the clearer I see that our original sin—which isn't really a sin—is evolving the mind too much and into the dead end of a vicious circle. The human mind has the capacity to mold and shape our perception almost without limits, and we start to forget which parts are the reality and which are the projections. True enough, they seem so inextricably intertwined that it's hard to tell them apart—or so it appears. But that in itself is merely a projection and is only as true as much as we believe it is. As primal explorers, we are always perfectly capable of discerning between the spirit-based reality and the mind-based overlays on top of it.

Another illusion-turned-delusion is our mock insistence to get to the bottom of everything in our lives. We end up being trapped in our quasi search for the Truth, over which we are too often willing to fight to the death. We keep forgetting that we can only ever see our side of the truth.

As humans, we may have reached a point where our lives are completely controlled by the mind, yet we fiercely cling to the illusion of exercising our free will. We are stubborn when we believe that we are not in denial. With all of our energy, we resist the very liberation we seek.

Yet I say: we just don't know better. We can't, because the only belief system that we trust is now skewed, usurped, and hijacked by a benevolent father—the mind, who merely wants what is the best for us, but will keep us grounded in the fake safety of our tiny, suffocating children's bedroom.

If each and every experience we have is filtered through and transformed by the mind, even the internal processes of introspection, is there anything at all we can rely on? How can we ever detect and unmask the deception and manipulation of the mind?

Before we tackle this trillion dollar question, let's both take another deep breath.

...

And even another.

...

Now let's close the eyes for a moment and feel the body.
Smile. Feel it in your heart.
Every chance we get, we can benefit so much from a simple pause like that. A breath, or two. Some feeling too. That, is already meditation.

And then there is more: we can go deeper, and truer. There are countless techniques out there to help us quiet the mind. Breathwork is my number one choice. But it can be anything, as long as it's the real deal—and for me, that means only one thing: the Spirit *moving* through us. That's the only awakening or enlightenment there is. The rest is a dream within a dream.

Our essence, the soul, is the Spirit that permeates our being—which is both our body and our energy field. Not only is the soul what keeps us alive at any given moment, it is also what can make us conscious, present, and aware.

How do you know you are alive? Descartes said, "I think, therefore I am." Whether he was talking about thinking or something else, perhaps knowing or being aware, that is now lost in time and translation. My intuition is informing me that he was walking the edge between the mind and awareness, but the pull of his focus kept deporting him back to his old story. I choose to believe this intuitive message, because I'm not really invested in being right or wrong and that makes me free in this regard. I'm aware there is no finality of truth to it anyway.

As a primal explorer, how do *you* know you're alive?

If we open our eyes now and look around, it is more than obvious that we're alive! Look, my fingers are typing and I feel the chair I'm sitting on. You see these words in front of you clear as day, you're aware of your breathing, and perhaps also of your thinking.

But how is that different from a dream? How can you be sure your whole life and this reality, as we call it, is not an illusion? Is there a way to know for certain?

We all have experienced that immersement in a dream so true that we're shocked when we wake up from it. A moment ago, we could have sworn the dream, with all its powerful sensations, feelings, emotions, thoughts, beliefs, desires, and choices, was real, the *only* Reality there was. But only when we actually awaken and experientially compare the two states as we phase out of one and into the other, can we realize the relative difference between a mere dream and our *true reality*!

Or is it really *true*?

In the same vein, one who awakens from the all-encompassing hold of the mind into a more expansive state of awareness, can tell that, well, something is going on. This is far from being black and white, and there are layers and quantum superpositions to it all, which the mind polarizes into a dichotomy of true-false, right-wrong, and ultimately good-evil extremes.

What is of key importance and can make a difference, is that we can practice and train the awakening of awareness. We get *better* at it. Once you awaken from either a dream or the grasp of the mind, you'll only remember the fresh knowing of the relative difference between the before and after states for a short time, until that awareness slips through the bone fingers of your attention. But that brief time will gradually get longer and our memory of true awareness will remain more faithful to the original, as we keep awakening, day by day, meditation by meditation, breath by breath.

This practice is the reason I love breathwork meditation. You see, the point of meditation—when you are training the awakening of awareness—is not merely to relax and feel better. Understand that we are not training in the technique of meditation in order to improve its execution. We are training to deliberately release all control and lose our daily grip on awareness—as well as then being able to re-awaken out of it. We are training awakening, not awareness—which, or should we say, who, can't really be trained. Our practice entails losing ourselves before knowing ourselves.

Why would you do that? What is driving you, motivating you? Why would you want to awaken from a dream?

Only you can know that, for yourself. So ask yourself—not because you're looking for an answer, but because that is the training. And that is circular too.

Building on the knowing and *not knowing* of who you are, let's—yeah—take a deep breath, inviting in a quick flash of intuition about the simple question related to this chapter's title: *what are we doing here?*

...

My own answer this time was quite straightforward: I'm here to help lessen the suffering in the world in a sustainable manner, by awakening from the mind.

We choose to trust our intuition. It tells us who we are right now, at this moment. We may never again be exactly this. Ah, the value of transience!

The mind will want to identify with at least some of it. Thoughts will cavort in our heads, "Am I this mind, am I the Buddha, or this body, the human suit? Am I eternal awareness, the soul? Maybe a mix of it all, or something else entirely? I'm confused. How can I be certain? It's scary to not know..." Et cetera, ad nauseam.

How can I know what I am doing here if I don't even know who I am?

Remember: all of it, a dream. Beyond it, in the void before the creation of whatever we want, exists a choice, a leap of faith.

Now tell me, what *are* you doing here?

What do you *want*?

"Our free will is not truly ours if it's not most deeply in tune with the Universe."
—Ink by Star, Book 11: *Cancer*

WAKING UP

Let me ask you another thing: how do you fall asleep? What procedure do you follow to get there?

I'm not talking about the little rituals that make it easier to calm down before bedtime. I'm asking *what exactly do you do internally a moment before you lose consciousness?*

If you don't know, you can simply try finding out tonight. Observe yourself when you go to bed. Remain present with everything going on within for as long as you can. But maybe that will prevent you from falling asleep? Nah, I doubt it.

Even if you already know the answer, I believe there is always another layer to everything. Perhaps I can motivate you to go deeper and unmask the mind's attempt to explain the inexplicable.

My intuitive observations, based not solely on the mind but on my gathered experience beyond it, tell me that we can learn a lot about the awakening of awareness by consciously exploring how we fall asleep.

One might then ask, what about how we wake up?

That is what we'll now use as the primal explorer's proving ground.

> "Awakening is not linear, it is holographic."
> —Ink by Star, Book 4: *Cygnus*

Diesel mind

One curious, quite early morning, I woke up to nothing.

I mean, nothing special was happening around me, no sounds or people were present, everything was still, and I had no good reason to awaken. I opened my eyes, saw the ceiling of my bedroom, and that was it.

There followed a prolonged moment of internal silence. I had no way of gauging how long it lasted, nor did I even consider wanting to. My focus was glued to the sensation of inner nothingness.

I wasn't trying to do anything, neither to extend this state, nor to snap out of it. I didn't care, on a level that I only knew from my previous experience of *stopping the world*. I didn't know the concept of *caring* or *wanting*. At the same time, I was fully present, conscious and aware—depending on the definitions of these words—to which I'll circle back later.

The first non-neutral feeling was a rising curiosity.

Thoughts rushed into the void:

"What?"

"What is this?"

"What is going on?"

There was no one home, though, nobody to provide an-swers—the usual answers I'd been accustomed to. The thoughts shrugged their metaphorical shoulders and drifted on and by, phasing out of my focus.

A sensation of fascination, awe, and mystery permeated me. Note that I am deliberately not saying permeated *my mind*, because my intuition sourced the sensations from everywhere, all around—I couldn't even tell whether they were inside or outside of me or whether they were mine or not.

Even though I was somehow able to *read* thoughts cruising by and through my field of presence, I wasn't *thinking* them. They were definitely not part of me the same way my knowing was. Like emotions and feelings, these thoughts were signals, units of information left open to a consequent interpretation, separate from my true core as I was aware of it.

In retrospect, I can estimate that state lasted for less than a minute, roughly. The time flew, not unlike the way it passes in dreams. But that is of no significance to the intention of this chapter. I only mention it to placate the mind a little, to give it a bone to occupy itself with—and also as a token of my gratitude to the mind for having patience with this subject at hand. I believe we're in this together, the mind and I, so I want to develop a beautiful friendship here.

At one point, with no volition on my part and without any-thing meaningful happening externally, my state of inner silence ended. It was as if a specific, albeit otherworldly resource had been spent: I ran out of some cosmic fuel—something I had experienced before when dreaming awake.

Without much exaggeration, I tell you that it felt as if a fantastical, quiet, yet powerful diesel engine fired up in my head. A distinct counterpoint to the subtle, gossamer cosmic instrument that I was and had experienced seconds ago, this interloper grabbed my atten-tion and outmuscled the ethereal. First, I heard a murmur in my bones, a tremor which grew to a steady humming vibration—and voilà, I was back to my normal self!

All the thoughts, hovering aimlessly a moment ago in the absence of a leader, snapped to attention and made sense again in their usual, rational manner. The questions were answered again, answers then immediately doubted, giving rise to a chain of emotions and feelings in the body. The whole old game was afoot once more.

On another occasion, I woke up in the morning and I couldn't move. My eyes were open and I saw everything in my field of vision normally: the white sheets on the bed, the pillow, the nightstand with books on it, the walls with pictures, the doors, the ceiling. But I couldn't move any part of my body. It didn't feel as if my body was paralyzed or otherwise made rigid—there just wasn't any control of it coming from my volition.

At first, I believed I was having a slightly ominous, weird dream. However, every detail of the bedroom I inspected was so real and stable, without that shifty, ever-changing quality of a dream. And it was all so contemporary, embedded in the present time just as it should be. I mean, I was fully aware that it should be morning and that I should be waking up in my bed with my girlfriend already gone.

In a peculiar way, I was still able to think. I sensed a subtle difference between the normality I was used to in my head and the external reality. I couldn't move, but all else seemed the same as always.

This experience happened during the time in my life just after I had started experimenting with dreaming awake, when I was still trying to find my hands in my dreams. I had read in one of Castaneda's books that something like this could happen.

In that book, don Juan informs Carlos Castaneda that experiencing this kind of paralysis is brought about by a shift of one's awareness into the dreaming body before one learns how to intentionally cross back into the physical body. He claims it isn't dangerous per se, but warns that one can still easily die of fright. The trick is not to obsess or make a big drama of it.

For some inexplicable reason, the emotions I felt were as far from fear as possible. I was elated by my accomplishment! The experience I had was proof that it was all real and attainable—even for me. It felt like a promise of great things to come. I just wanted to stay there, fully immersed, present, and savor as much of that sweet, mysterious nectar as I could.

It didn't last long. Honestly, I don't remember exactly how that state ended, but I believe I lost consciousness for a moment, probably just falling asleep, and the next instant I was awake again, lying in the same position—but now I could move normally.

I had yet another profound experience of losing consciousness when I broke my wrist at the age of fifteen. On a grand summer day, we were celebrating the closure of a week-long computer graphics course by having a lively outdoor picnic. We were having great fun, but as I went to fetch my printouts, something less pleasant occurred. As I was returning to the picnic site, running around a corner, I bumped into someone coming the other way, and my right hand, holding a stack of printouts, was caught and pressed hard in a weird position between our bodies.

The accident didn't seem serious at first. I apologized to my colleague for having crashed into him, and picked up the printouts that had fallen to the ground. Returning to my seat at the dining table, I gobbled up the grilled meat still waiting on my plate. It was only as I sat there, lounging in the sun and sipping my soda, that I realized my wrist hurt. An unusual bump was gently protruding and it all felt as if it was in the wrong place, on top of which, it moved around and retracted as I pressed on it, trying to put it back in its correct position.

A rush of panic enveloped me. I became suddenly aware that something bad was happening, but the mind still wanted to deny it. I felt heat rising to my head and I became weak and scared. But my social fear of speaking out and asking for help was greater than the pain. I kept glancing at my teacher, who was sitting right across from me, and imagined the dreaded scenario of how I'd open up and admit to my injury. I had always been most afraid of demanding somebody's attention and wasting their time, and an insistent, tiny voice whispered in my head that I was just not worthy of being assisted. Yet I knew I'd have to face the horror of speaking up—sooner or later. My indecisiveness was agonizing.

At the height of my nightmare, something in me made a choice, and I impulsively called out my teacher's name, not yet knowing what I was going to say to him. I simply leapt to a decision, because I had to.

From that moment on, everything unfolded pretty quickly and smoothly. Almost immediately, I felt immense relief. My teacher kindly drove me to a nearby hospital where an X-ray confirmed that one of the small bones in my wrist was broken and a surgical resetting of the bone had to be done. I was asked to wait for the procedure, and my teacher waited with me—actually, he stayed there the whole time, metaphorically holding my hand, because my parents had gone away for the week on summer holiday.

Soon enough, I lay on an operating table and the nurse was about to administer anesthesia.

I was afraid.

What if it doesn't take?

What if I remain fully conscious and I feel everything, but I'm unable to move or talk?

With my usual luck around health, something is bound to go wrong...

I despaired.

Too young to dare oppose the authority of doctors in any way, I resigned myself to whatever would happen to me.

The nurse put a mask over my nose and mouth and told me to relax and breathe in the sleeping gas slowly and naturally.

I did my best to follow that order.

Nothing happened.

I remained completely present and certain that my consciousness would just not go away.

I prayed that the nurse or the doctor would notice how awake I still was, and stop the procedure.

Surely they must have had cases like this before, and they are prepared. There must be a protocol for this. They must know what they're doing.

The doctor approached without even glancing in my direction. He was holding something in his hand. I didn't want to move to look. With all of my focus and will, I just wanted to go under, now!

Then the gas started to work.

Something in my head began to spin, slowly at first, like a washing machine on a slow setting. I closed my eyes firmly and actively tried to fall asleep.

The spinning got faster and faster. I wasn't entirely certain whether I felt it in my head, or if it was happening externally. At one point, I thought I saw a small tornado, a twister, lurking right above my body...

I must be seeing things.

The thought made me happy and I finally felt optimistic about my ordeal. Then I became curious, but also partially scared of going under too deep.

The spinning phenomenon grabbed all of my attention. A deep hum emanated from the movement, but there was nothing moving. At each full turn of that cycling void, a single vibrational blip was emitted, the sound of which reminded me of computer games. The frequency of the rotations increased to the point where I couldn't count them any longer and the blips started to melt together, clicking like a radiation detector in a danger zone.

I felt as if my being was curling unto itself, twisting around almost like chewing gum, extending longer and thinner, yet at the same time I sensed that my body was not involved at all. It was like a dream, but different.

The intense spinning accelerated even more—if that was at all possible—and the blips changed into simpler ticks, sounding like *taks*. Strangely though, the faster they went, the slower they were.

The energy of the non-existing movement was reaching cosmical proportions and was about to explode into a supernova, but the *taks*, now clicks, became sporadic, almost random.

At one point, I viscerally felt a *tak* and a click shifting into a subtle tug somewhere in my body. At first, I believed I felt it in my stomach, but then it repeated and continued in my right wrist, as if something was pulling and pushing it, yanking it forcefully, and tinkering with it in some unnatural way.

This only lasted for a second, or so it seemed, then all hell broke loose, cliché or not...

Vomit, suffocation, puke, cough explosion, dread, life, pain, birth, naked presence, helplessness, confusion, giving in, letting go!

I came to, realizing I was leaning over the left side of the cart I had been placed onto after the procedure, and I was barfing out whatever remained of the picnic food.

My teacher stood up from his waiting room bench and approached me, smiling reassuringly. His energy was full of caring. That was all the comfort I needed in order to know everything was alright.

Thank you, dear friend!

Unusual and downright mind-boggling as those events were, they were pale in comparison to my experience of *stopping the world*. I can put them into the same group with many other instances of extraordinary states and shifts of consciousness, including meditation, but in all those cases, the mind was merely subtly altered, or paused, or asleep, whereas when I *stopped the world*, the mind was no longer there. It was absolutely gone as if it had never existed.

But what does that even mean?

"Light is visible only when it touches something."
—Ink by Star, Book 12: *Leo*

WHAT IS THE MIND?

Can you catch a thought?

Forget for a moment all that you think you know about the brain, the neurotransmitters, the chemical and quantum science about our thinking enigma. Not that the above doesn't matter—but we're primal explorers now, remember?

We're interested in the experience here—however subjective—more than just the theory.

So let's dive into our own mind! Turn on the headlights of attention and let's observe, carefully and sincerely, all that we can witness going on within.

To orient ourselves, as a point of reference, let's start by noticing our bodies. I can feel my feet touch the floor. My thighs are generally relaxed, with a tinge of nervousness upon being "tested" like this. A deep breath introduces a new wave of presence. My shoulders rise with my chest and remain straighter than usual as I focus there. The exhaled air caresses my nostrils.

The senses gather information, yes. I hear music playing in the background. I see the letters and words being typed on my computer screen, and beyond that, I see the walls, the windows, and the trees swaying in the morning autumn wind. I smell the intense scent of an incense stick that has almost finished burning. All of this comes together in the field of my consciousness and creates my reality as it is: this moment.

But where *am* I? Am I inside my head, or somewhere else? Am I observing the world from behind my eyes? Am I a tiny person, located in the center of my dull-gray brain?

Who is thinking this?

And most importantly: what is *this*? How can I define a thought? Can I perceive it better, clearer? Can I slow it down and decipher it, analyze it, control it?

What is the thought made of? Is it digital? Energetic? Magical?

Are thoughts speaking the same language I do? Am I translating in the process? Can a thought exist without a form, a structure, without syntax? Without meaning? Is that still a thought then?

It's complex, isn't it? Overwhelming!

All these questions... But remember: as primal explorers, we're not really after answers. We're exploring the potentialities, freely, with our awareness, opening up to whatever seems incredible, savoring the process. We're making it up as we go. We're creating.

Let's refocus: what do I want here? I want to understand thinking!

From what I can tell, thinking is almost like water, or air, constantly twirling and changing, never at peace or still. Elusive, fluid, untouchable.

I see, as a primal explorer who could very well be wrong, that thoughts are everywhere, an endless stream—or perhaps an ocean, spilling over the boundaries, through time, tense, and sense, ceaselessly, carelessly. Not fish, but jellyfish. How can I catch one to put it under a microscope? Maybe I can't.

Without a context, thoughts are chaotic. Order must come from outside, a priori.

When I engage with my thinking, I believe that I can either follow a strict procedure, like a railway track for the train of thoughts to run on, or I can somehow call up and invoke a more transcendental mold to welcome and guide the thoughts passing by my window of attention, without actually ever controlling them.

The former is a linear process where we add to an existing body of knowledge, build science rationally, and direct thoughts by filtering them through a sieve of expectations and interpretations. The latter is a matter of awareness.

As the mind observes itself in the linear manner, it enters a circular loop of endless confusion, a recursive trap that renders us incapable of distinguishing between reality and interpretation—if we are without awareness, that is. But as soon as we awaken to awareness, we see it all. And that is our birthright, our sacred duty and our destiny: to awaken!

But to reach and realize that, we need to want it first.

The earnest desire to awaken awareness is something we can train, not unlike a muscle. It is only when we sincerely want our awakening, that we can truly do something about it in practice. Instead of merely thinking about it, we do it and experience it. We walk the path. That's what counts here. I call this meditation, but you can call it by another name—that doesn't matter, as long as you keep doing it.

If you have been paying close attention, you will have noticed that I didn't really provide an answer to "what is the mind?" or "what is a thought?" I don't want to add to the mind-based vocabulary—even if I had anything to offer. My intuition is clearly guiding me to take another approach and boldly go where no one has gone... Well, you know. A bit of my nerdy humor here.

Perhaps you can feel the same way I do: that it is ultimately not so important to understand everything. Some things may be beyond mental comprehension anyway, and our obsession with having to dissect, know, and control may be the root of our many problems on this marvelous blue planet of ours.

What if this "mindful" vicious cycle is controlling human values and setting our priorities? Do we need the mind so highly evolved? But the mind insists! The mind itself—whatever we say and mean that it is—has convinced us we need it, desperately, more and more and ever more. For the mind, it is never enough. That's why we never pause and release control. The mental scientist in us—as opposed to the primal explorer—keeps us focused on developing the mind alone. Ironically, as complete, magical beings, we managed to evolve the mind probably far beyond its original purpose and into something we don't even need, to the point it has become a burden and a hindrance, our downfall. That was our collective free will choice.

And now, as complete, magical beings, we can choose to outcreate our own mess and transmute this over-developed mind into something unprecedented, unconditionally loving and all-inclusive.

It's time we become a new brand of scientists: soul scientists! How?

"A confused mind is best cleared by being left alone."
—Ink by Star, Book 15: *Scorpius*

Breathwork

Breathwork is the go-to meditation practice for me.

I've written extensively about breathwork practice in my other books and I talk about it countless times when leading workshops and events. This time, I'll try a novel approach in tune with the nature of our adventure here: being primal explorers and soul scientists. Let's dive straight into the essence of it.

Actually, before we do, let me reveal an innocent subterfuge I've been using in this book so far. The book is organized in a way that chapters somewhat alternate between theory and stories, with some primal exploration in between. I wanted to give the mind many opportunities to pause, relax, and perhaps even begin transmuting into something brand new. When I say that, what I mean is that I want us to outcreate our *linear, looping mind* and let our *true mind* take over and grok the meaning of all this in a way never before experienced.

Ultimately, to emerge from the circular collective daydream we all share, we must take a leap of faith. But what does this mean? This leap is huge. It's larger than we know. It's on par with dying. It can't be anything less if we want to transcend all we know and have kept repeating our whole life. This leap of faith is so unknowable that there is no way of talking about it, except in a roundabout, allegorical manner—which is perfectly good enough for us.

Moreover, there will be many leaps, not just one. On many levels. One leap of faith is happening just now: as I am writing this and you are reading it. We both must believe—and *feel*—that something monumental is going on here that will change our lives, even if this is just one baby step or if we're only planting a seed.

The key is the passion with which we instill our presence at this moment!

From this passion, our focus spreads and envelops our whole being. Possibilities open up just like miracles bound to happen at long last. Life is a mystery! We haven't yet witnessed all there is to it, far from it. What if a dream we've been awaiting for many lifetimes is knocking on your door right now? Can you hear it?

Shall we open the door?

Breathwork practice is a continuous effort of faith-leaping. It never gets boring as we never exhaust our potential of expansion.

In essence, with breathwork we are pausing the linear mind and allowing our belief system to invite our soul to enter deeper and lovelier into our being. We experience that as a powerful vibration, made of silence. The resistance we may encounter can be used as fuel for more self-love discipline. We keep practicing daily and training our awareness.

This is a practical chapter, so let me describe what happened to me last night during my breathwork. Mind you, I've been practicing for ten years and have done hundreds if not thousands of breathwork meditations by now. Yet without exaggeration, I can claim that my experience yesterday was probably more profound than ever before and has cleared something in me to a further degree. Right on time for me to write about it, too!

"The only way out of your head is into your body."
—Ink by Star, Book 14: *Libra*

A way through

My recording of choice was David Elliott's specialized breathwork meditation on abuse, addiction, and creative obligation. I had experienced many cravings throughout the day and my linear mind was insisting I wouldn't be able to do a decent breathwork because of my weakened state, which was now infused with guilt, remorse, and doubt. But I knew better.

Each of David's recordings consisted of two parts: the introduction and the meditation. Having listened to that introduction many times, I could have skipped it—but I never did. In fact, a huge amount of my practice was already done during the introduction: I took time for myself and relaxed, and got inspired and moved by both David's insights and the neutral, loving way he delivered them. I always felt that we were all in the same boat. My intention for the practice strengthened and sharpened and my heart started opening.

Like every time, burning a leaf of sage helped my linear mind trust the ritual by believing the space was being cleansed and the healing was commencing. I also gently sprayed the room and myself with David's unique Sanity mix, and applied a drop of his Open Heart essential oil blend.

Lying down on my back, I placed a light weight over my sternum to help me focus my attention on the heart—something I don't always do. As usual, I then covered myself with a lavender-scented eye pillow. In my hands, I squeezed my trusty ocean stones that I held throughout my breathing. Following the directions on the recording, I proceeded to breathe exclusively through my mouth in a special rhythm: two inhales, one exhale.

The first seven or eight breaths felt almost like diving into the slightly cold water of a lake. Courage flowed through my veins and my determination to breathe was rock solid. Just like warming up in sports, I started gaining momentum. I had only just begun, after all.

Then saliva formed in my throat and as I tried to inhale through the mouth with my usual force, I choked. Coughing out a few times, I returned to the breathing rhythm, but the mind wasn't happy. It started to nag, as it does, about my bad luck or whatever was the cause for my choking accident. It just shouldn't have happened. Something was broken now. Everything seemed lost.

As I worked hard to get free of the saliva in my throat, a gigantic temptation to stop the breathwork overwhelmed me, but I checked myself. Staying aware, I didn't choose to believe the voice in my head at all. Instead of listening to the mind's desperate insistence that I clear out all of the remaining saliva from my throat and mouth, I started to let go of control. I didn't want to care any longer. If I choked again, I'd simply cough, then breathe on. Wouldn't even matter.

What did matter was to feel the body. Each breath, lifting the diaphragm, the opening up of the stomach and then the chest as the first inhalation crossed my heart, bringing the energy and emotions upwards, ever upwards, and then the second inhalation that ascended all the way into my shoulders, filling me up with elation and clarity.

Then, exhalation. Ah, the exhalation! Just letting it all go, out, away... But not throwing it away—on the contrary, reconnecting it to the whole, the Universe, the Source. The breath returning to its rightful, sacred owner: the Spirit.

Inhaling into my stomach, inhaling into the top of my chest, exhaling slowly yet deliberately.

Repeating.

On and on.

Minutes passed.

Then, my feet got restless.

Even more restless...

Like so many times before, I just couldn't fully relax, no matter how hard I tried. And the less I could relax, the harder I was trying, until it completely absorbed me to the point of obsession.

It was the same routine every time this came up.

Why is this always happening to me? Why me? What am I doing wrong, again? Is it something I have eaten? Is it the way I succumb to the many addictions I never seem to be able to finally quit? What is broken in me, really?

I decided to push all these assailing thoughts away and breathe on.

Let's think of nothing, I thought.

Calm down, I told myself. *Just relax. You can do it.*

Aw, man, if only these feet would stop bothering me for just one minute! What the hell! Please, just stop. Why don't you?!?

At this point, I was kicking with my feet like a petulant child.

Aargh!

No. Stop fighting. Just breathe. Forget it. It's nonsense. It's a trap. It always happens. But why? What am I doing wrong? How do I stop this? When, when, when will I be good enough for this to stop bothering me?

I bent my legs at the knees and increased my effort to try to relax. *Legs, leggo!!! Damn you, legs!* I extended them again only to bend them back, then kicked them out as if to break a wall casing me in!

Fuck-ing-knees!

RELAX!!!

I had ants or worse in my lower legs, and my knees particularly. Nervous feet, I called them.

But I knew… I knew then that it was all just a consequence of a great confusion, an upheaval in the mind. I really needed to get out of my head and enter my heart. But how?

Do this. Do that. Meditate. Meditate. Meditate. Stop thinking.
Nothing helped. Nothing.
If only just…
Aaargh!!!

A fury of frustrated, unexpressed sadness enveloped me with the speed of a dark, massive stormcloud shrouding the sun and dimming the light.

I kicked my feet in crazy frustration. I was enraged, I would break everything in the world if I could. But that rage was not as strong as the sense of futile helplessness, utter weakness, and chronic powerlessness. I was rendered docile and passive to the point I found myself in a vicious cycle of despising myself. I shrank into a small and worthless nobody and I simply stopped caring entirely about what would happen to me or my breathwork.

I stopped breathing—well, I resumed breathing naturally: one breath in, one breath out.

I gave up…

I actually wanted myself to fail. Miserably.

I wanted to die.

Ah, the drama…

And then I remembered!

This was it! Yes! I had just experienced a loss of awareness, that was all. No biggie.

I *woke* up.

Instantly, all was clear again. I realized exactly what had been going on in my head: how one voice in the mind had ever so subtly convinced me to believe such dire negativity. Out of nothing, it had constructed a dark image of my unworthiness that in turn gave rise to hopeless feelings that had taken over my whole mood and perception of my life. Well, not exactly out of nothing.

This, whatever it is, this voice in the mind—and please bear with me as I will do my best to explain it in the coming paragraphs below—always rides on something prior, something negative we used to believe in the past. It grabs our old attention that was focused on darkness and spins it around like a masterful go player, using it against us.

Ultimately, it doesn't matter what reasons or argumentation it uses. It's like a nightmare, which never makes sense after we wake up from it. However, when we are in the midst of its hypnotic power, we sincerely believe that it *does* make sense. Even the most absurd ideas pass by our radar of normality.

Let's consider, as primal explorers, what *is* sense?

When we believe that something makes sense, so it does, by definition. There is no absolute test for what makes sense and there is no final authority that could either confirm or reject our sense against what we believe.

We define what makes sense to us on the fly, by creating the arbitrary mental definitions needed to convince ourselves—and we call those the *truth*. This happens when we argue our viewpoints and beliefs and fight with others about them. We may believe we are stating facts, but are we really?

This is an important idea to open up to. For a scientific society, it's hard to accept that facts and truth are complex notions, just like mind and awareness, and that our whole grasp of reality may indeed be flimsy in some circular manner, and perhaps impossible to ever fully understand.

Yet we don't even have to understand anything in order to believe in it and thus create and build our total subjective reality. Such is our power of creation—and the irony lies in that this voice usurps our own power and hijacks and abuses it for its own sinister purposes.

But why would this voice want to do that to us?

What *is* this voice?

Well, that's the million dollar question, ain't it? Joking aside, tell me: what do *you* think this voice is?

I simply call it the voice of *miscreation*.

I don't want to dwell on it for too long, so let me just say that as we focus our creativity in a sustained manner on something, we imbue it with our life force energy. In a way, we make it real. We bring it to life. When our sustained focus has been directed against ourselves and against our greater good, we can become quite destructive and what we then create is still a bundle of our own energy, but it is sort of getting a life of its own—which I call a miscreation.

The miscreation lives on within us, feeding off our negativity, our self-destruction, and our lack of self-love. Working through the mind—which is a kind of energetic amplifier and interpreter—the miscreation uses a voice of digital, linear reason to convince us, time and again, to believe and follow its bidding. But it was us who originally programmed the miscreation that way, when we first created it. We gave it its life purpose, which is so utterly destructive to ourselves.

In a flash of intuition, I first called this voice of miscreation the *overmind*, because it seemed to me that it covers over the true reality with a veneer of misdirection or illusion, like an overcoat. I could just as well call it an *undermind*, as it undermines our clarity and our best efforts of understanding life. But perhaps the most neutral and generic term would be the *submind*.

This submind is a digital, dualistic subset of our linear, logical mind—which itself has its own important function for human beings and humanity, and is in turn a part of our holistic, non-linear, soul mind, which I may also call our true mind.

The submind has one particular attribute: it is so self-absorbed that it keeps circling back to its own projections, thus strengthening them in the process. It is super susceptible to any emotional influence. It is flimsy in its capacity of being consistent, and this openness and lack of rigidity actually makes it a great support tool for our creativity, imagination, and fantasy. However, this inconsistency can also make it extremely prone to manipulation coming from the miscreation.

The submind is more than just an inert thought structure. It is an active, ongoing loop that permeates the mind through and through, and is therefore able to override it completely, by constantly shouting the most negative criticisms of yourself, over every other thought and sentiment you have.

When hijacked by the miscreation, the submind becomes a deceptive layer miscreated over the top of our mind. It becomes the ultimate trickster, a champion of logical nonsense, a masterful cheating chess player. It will always find a way to crack our every mental defense by saying whatever we need to hear to get us to believe the most insensitive and convoluted lies.

Why would we keep believing whatever negativity the submind of the miscreation keeps spouting at us? Why would we ever trust any of it? Again, it's circular. In fact, it's the very definition of a vicious circle. The more we believe it, the more we feed it, and the more we become it.

Is the miscreation, with its submind, evil? Are we, human beings, evil? Well, what I see is merely a temporary loss of awareness. A part of us—the miscreation—gets entangled in ideas isolated from the reality of Mother Nature and that causes us all this pain. On top of that, the miscreation creates in us the illusion of suffering.

So during that breathing session, finally awake once again, with my complete awareness of what was going on, I knew exactly what I had to do in order to keep opening and awakening: simply keep on breathing, nothing more.

Without any mind-based doubt, I knew that as I breathed on, I would encounter great resistance. The only way through resistance is to be aware of it, knowing it is simply the mind—the sub-mind—trying to control the experience. You should never engage or reason with it. Simply be aware it is a resistance and return to the breath.

The only job you have is to breathe. Feel it in the body. Breathe in, breathe out. It is super simple. Don't let the mind tell you otherwise.

Remember this every time when you breathe and forget again. Remember it over and over. To remember, you will need to awaken, but it is super easy. You are just breathing. It's not rocket science. You don't need to control it. Just do it. That's all there is to it. Take breaths and feel your body as you do. Don't focus on anything else. If you do it for a long enough time, your brain will pause. The mind will go away. You will vibrate. I promise you.

So breathing on, again in the proper breathwork pattern, my awareness expanded again. Cutting like a laser beam through the veil of illusion the miscreation had been spinning, I reached a perfect knowing. This quantum enlightenment is actually a remembering of who we truly are, an awakening within the dream that is life.

From there on, the road was clear and easy, lovable.

Inhaling into my stomach, inhaling into the top of my chest, exhaling freely and completely: pure sunlight!

Repeating.

Within minutes, an inner smile formed within my tingling chest. My heart was opening.

Yes, I know: my heart was not literally opening up and bleeding out all over my internal organs. If you believe in the chakras or energetic centers in a human body, you can imagine such a spinning vortex of energy becoming even more vibrant and free to rotate. A magnetic love field moved through my awareness and I felt an electric current oscillating gently in my nervous system. Or you can imagine that my endocrine gland, called the thymus, accelerated its hormone secretion and caused me to feel all emotional inside in a great way, expanding my viewpoints, growing my will and willingness and thus helping me to face with grace whatever problems in life were out there.

What we believe, doesn't matter. It's arbitrary, at best. What matters is that we are aware with crystal clarity that we have the power to choose what we believe.

Breathing on like that for maybe six more minutes, the vibration in my body increased. My hands were tingling in a pleasant, safe way. A mild humming trembled all around my heart area, feeling liberating and promising.

With each breath, I relaxed deeper. There was nothing else in my field of perception other than the immediacy of my abdomen and upper chest rising and falling continuously. The vibration became so strong that I felt as if a powerful electric current was running through me. It was charging me with my own life force.

The head was becoming clearer and also more confused at the same time, depending on my viewpoint. I felt as if one side of me was losing ground to another, older, wiser, and infinitely more real version of myself.

The confusion I experienced was the curious lack of my well-known ongoing linear transcription of life, as if the narrator that normally explained the world in every detail had suddenly gone silent. It was only after it was gone that I could grasp that the usual narrative had been prejudiced and righteous to the extreme, leaving no space for any alternative.

In that absence, or void, I didn't feel alone or frightened. On the contrary, I was filled with the presence of a new kind of aliveness that made all the sense in the world!

Clarity came over me. You could call it a prophetic vision or a blast of pure faith, but no words can do justice to its reality. It would have to be experienced firsthand in order to ever be grokked. Yes, *grok* is a real word, and a most appropriate one at this place—feel free to look it up.

After the breathwork, I recorded what I was feeling and also re-ceiving as a message. You might notice a subtle difference in the voice of my writing for the rest of this chapter. The message was coming through me in a state of mental silence, and as a cosmic interpreter, I translated it into words.

What was this state I was experiencing? Quite honestly, it's truly indescribable, and we would probably have to create yet another new word for it, but even that wouldn't help, because how would one describe the unknowable?

Lacking a better term, I just call it awareness, or awakened awareness, or perhaps consciousness, and the process of getting there is what I call awakening or quantum enlightenment. The terms don't even matter. What matters is that you do your work and create that experience for yourself, not once, but many, many times.

I'd even venture to claim that it is vital to do this daily. The meditation works when the mind stops and you feel your own vibration flowing through your body. If you don't feel the vibration, then the mind is still controlling you. You need to do it daily because it adds up. It's cumulative, and it's healing.

When you vibrate, you believe you are healing. Even if it is the placebo effect, which arguably is all we've got anyway, it is still healing. We are our own healers and creators of our reality, whether you call it a placebo or not.

In order to create, you need to vibrate.

If you don't do it daily you will get progressively more and more lost in the submind, without even noticing. The submind will have you believe you are doing something beneficial for your overall healing, but you are not. If you are vibrating daily, you will know that.

So don't lose this awareness. Leave yourself a note. Make it a routine. Do *whatever it takes*, and meditate and vibrate daily. It is vital. It is the single most important thing in your life.

If you vibrate every day, your mind will eventually go away—in a good way. You will have vanquished the submind. It will feel confusing—almost like dying, I suppose. You will lose all your bearings. It is the beginning of a new you. Of a much more powerful life.

You will have to relearn everything. You will learn how to function without the mind as you know it—but remember, it's not even your proper, true mind, only an imposter.

You will become one with nature. You will be in a permanent state of meditation. Your choices will be aligned with the universe's. You will reach your complete potential. You will fulfill your mission in this lifetime.

Who knows: the tiny voice of your true mind may finally grow powerful! What mystery lies in there. Perhaps we do have a chance to grok everything, everywhere, all at once. I believe this may be the goal of being an individual human being. If you want to reach it, you have to meditate and vibrate daily until the submind goes away for good. If you don't meditate *every* day, it's still good. It's a process.

"It is how we are treating darkness that creates the light."
—Ink by Star, Book 13: *Virgo*

WHAT IS LIFE?

I used to think that I was shy with my words because I was scared of what others would think of me. But in recent years, as I've been learning to love myself better and sweeter, I don't care for approval that much. I feel brave and powerful enough that I can speak out and say anything at all. Yet still, I don't. I patiently censor myself, trying to remain neutral, balancing my responses between the countless extremes of various convictions I encounter in our modern life, and also between my own expression and silent contemplation. Why?

The reason is circular, like everything in this world. Dual mind will perceive everything as a polarity. To transcend the dual mind, as part of creating and using a new syntax, *neutrality* is key.

What is neutrality?

As primal explorers, we can feel into this right now. What I sense is that *not* taking sides at all is not what neutrality is—that's more like nihilism, bypassing, and denial—all at once. To me, a centered, awareness-based neutrality is taking *all* sides at once. The mind may struggle to interpret that and may even give up entirely—but that's exactly how we make space for the foundation of a new syntax.

As I write this book, not only do I choose words and meanings attentively to convey precisely what I wish, but I strive to imbue the whole adventure—even between the lines and beyond the edges of the total scope—with a fresh, neutral creation. I do feel and intuit it trickling steadily through my inner heart and into our universe. Respecting and perpetuating this balance of neutrality, I believe, is the only way we can ever help change the world...

So how do we embrace all the sides there are? By loving them without even knowing or understanding them. Love is magical in that respect: it doesn't need a reason to exist, or grounds to grow. Instantly it arrives and permeates everything at once.

You have the power to generate love right in your heart, at any time. We all do.

Try it. *Now* is the best time for that. Witness your own power of love.

...

Taking all sides at once by loving them demands our expansion into the heart on a *soullular* level. So in order to transcend the dual mind, we must create neutrality—by transcending the dual mind. It doesn't get much more circular than that!

Still, we'll do it—it's humanity's destiny. One day we will realize what it was that we've been doing all along. We weren't fighting *what is*, or even trying to change the world. We were just loving—everything. We couldn't care less about duality or the dual mind. Nothing to see here. Just fake popularity. Boring...

Why don't we focus straight on our love instead?

Love...

This calming fire, bringing us all together.

Love.

The ultimate equalizer and transmuter.

The awareness comes with the experience, not the idea.

What if we say that everything is the same? What do we mean by this? Linearly and logically, rephrasing it as "nothing is more or better than anything else," it could either mean that nothing matters or it could mean that everything matters. Now, as soul scientists and universal translators, let's put the sentiment into the meaning!

Feel into "nothing matters." Cold, disconnected, alien. The dual mind might label it superior, worthy, and transcendental, but perhaps we can witness it more plainly as being insensitive.

Do we want to be "spiritually detached" to the point of insensitivity? The dual mind might lead us to believe that God Almighty created the world of insensitivity. Because, the argument goes, how else could He allow for evil, violence, and suffering in the world?

But ask yourself, what kind of Creator do you want to believe in, from your heart? The one who would desensitize everything for the benefit of the end goal? Exitus acta probat? (I googled this in Latin.) Or does your heart want to believe in some other Creator?

Now, let's feel into "everything matters." Ahhh, so sweet, full of light, hope, and enchantment! Every small, tiny detail matters as if it were my child, my baby. It is a part of me, a part of the whole. It matters, because I see it, I feel it, I love it!

The difference between nothing and everything is love.

So "everything matters" is good and "nothing matters" is bad, correct?

And welcome to yet another turn of the spiral! For as long as we live as human beings, upholding and feeding the dual mind, there will be no end to usurpations of every possible interpretation of any meaning.

The mind will use our passion as fuel for religious or philosophical crusades, whether metaphorical or literal. Our very feelings, projected onto the polarizing dual mind, will deceive our cognition as soon as we lose our spirit-based awareness—the only true source of neutrality.

This chapter is all about neutrality.

The dual mind—the submind—will stop at nothing and will hijack everything—that's in its nature, beyond the good and evil. We can observe it and remain aware of it all. And then we can outcreate its workings by bringing neutrality to it. By feeling the unbiased, unconditional love in our hearts.

Ever since I can remember, I have deeply intuited a peculiar layer, a veneer on top of absolutely everything. It took me quite some time before I realized that not everyone can perceive this fateful coating that distorts the reality of our world.

Take anything and the submind will envelop it, enter its core, absorb it and transform it. I can constantly sense this ominous process going on. I sense that if humanity indeed happens to be in the midst of some great strife, learning, or expansion here in the universe, it is intrinsically related to this grand machination!

At the center of our evolution, healing, and awakening, lies the pure, neutral awareness of what is in fact going on beneath everything that we can fathom or believe.

What I believe is that each of us is the missing link, the unique piece of the cosmic puzzle. Our very existence and our particular, individual awareness and point of view are needed to complete the whole. I see no point or benefit to us perfectly agreeing with each other—that would be redundant. No need for our common understanding of anything. Mutual, heart-based respect and a kind disposition of compassion is enough. Apart from that, everyone may and should believe what we can and want, no more, no less.

Nevertheless, the truth of every individual is merely a rigid seed of growth that is limited—by their individuality. And our common fate is to expand forever, collectively. So we need to learn how to grow all of our seeds together unconditionally—only then will they blossom into infinity.

What am I saying? Let me refocus and rephrase myself.

I am saying that if we ever want to co-exist together in mutual love and respect, we must learn to neutralize the dual submind by training our awakening of awareness. In short: meditate daily.

I see no other way.

The human condition may seem dire, but there is a silver lining: there *is* a way, it works, and it is available to absolutely everyone for free, right now! Let's make a choice to transmute the vicious circle of our inner dialog into a virtuous spiral of our consciousness, and the whole of reality will follow.

It can be easy.

"The universal language is rooted in neutrality, not truth."
—Ink by Star, Book 21: *Pegasus*

Oɴᴇ–ᴍɪɴᴜᴛᴇ ᴍᴇᴅɪᴛᴀᴛɪᴏɴ

When I set out to exchange with a *one-minute meditation*, I don't prepare all that much. I sit up straight with an inner smile and close my eyes.

I start drawing in my first deep breath without hesitation, before even thinking to remember the right way of doing it. As I am slowly inhaling, I remind myself that I want to prolong the inhalation for a count of four. At the same time, an intuition lets me know beyond a doubt that my top priority is feeling my body from within, feeling my every organ and all the tissues, muscles, sinew, and bones: everything in there all at once.

It's a holistic feeling. I am not going through a list in the mind or checking off parts of my body. Quite the opposite: the mental instructions and supervision somehow dissolve and fade away without any deliberate effort on my part. I focus solely on my bodily feelings, whatever my attention is drawn to. It doesn't matter. I don't direct anything. I just am: patient, trusting, acquiesced.

When the breath is fully in, I pause and hold it within.

That moment of phasing from inhalation to stillness is a magical doorway of awareness—transitions like this always are.

Counting to four again, I let go even more completely.

When I say counting, you can imagine something other than numbers increasing in my thoughts. You know how we can instinctively grasp whether there are three apples on the table as opposed to four or just two. We don't count, we simply look and know. Well, that's the way I count to four—a knowing gently shifts from one to two to three to four; it flows like a river over four large whitish stones submerged in clear, cold water.

"Breath awakens awareness."
—Ink by Star, Book 19: *Pisces*

Becoming honest

While I'm holding my breath, the world outside of me stops. I can sense my heart murmuring and vibrating with glee. All the cells of my body sing along and I feel so healthy, strong, and well-rested.

I remember to smile imperceptibly.

Switching to exhaling, I reset my abstract clock.

I let go. I release everything, not differentiating between good or bad—just letting it all go out. Not in the sense of expecting to actually cut anything out of my life, or to change it. All I do is feel the sensation of releasing a grip that is ordinarily always turned on—in my head. The breath helps me soften the grip, open up a flow, and move it throughout myself. I flatten out.

In the next step, my breathing stops and all movement ceases. Only an undulation remains, a peaceful ocean surface in the sunlight.

Nothing matters.

Everything matters.

My vibration rises almost as if I had done a complete 30-minute breathwork meditation. I am aware that my energy constantly vibrates, and it is only when I suspend the mind that I can witness it.

In this airless space, a timelessness hangs, the opposite of hurry. A wholeness. Holiness.

The most natural thing for me is to seamlessly melt into my life.

At this point, there is nothing else to do.

But then, the time comes. To return. To repeat.

Like spinning a dialing knob a quarter of a full circle, I ascend to cycle two of four.

Inhaling again, thoughts assail me like insects in flight, buzzing all around, unexpectedly popping into my bubble of awareness, demanding a distraction. The conditioned flight or fight response is not an option. Neutrality is.

I manage to remain present and keep going.

Feeling happy about it, successful of sorts. Proud even. I am doing my job.

And it dawns on me!

I have lost my clarity of awareness without even noticing. Just like when falling asleep: now you're here, and now you're not. Instead of opening up and expanding in awareness, I was losing myself, shriveling to nothing. What I had believed was reality was in fact an all-encompassing illusion, getting more and more subtly deceitful.

Following my old breathing routine that had obviously become stale, all I had really ended up doing was ticking checkboxes on my well-meant to-do list: breathe in and count, check, wait, check, relax, check, awaken some more, check. But those checks had unintentionally turned into white lies.

I wasn't awakening at all. My awareness was getting lost. I was selling my soul to the devil of duality for a sense of mock achievement of something I knew I was supposed to accomplish.

I was rushing to complete the task of meditating, while in the background—without even knowing—I was still placing ultimate importance on the miscreation energies, thus falling prey to my underlying sense of being powerless, my deeply rooted fear of rejection, and my constant need to prove my worth.

Without realizing, I had treated my meditation as a nuisance, a mere distraction on my way to what truly mattered, and I just wanted to be quickly done with it.

And that, just that, is to me the epitome of true meditation: the *clear honesty* of acknowledging such a loss of awareness.

In fact, it is the same thing as grounding, but at this point I want to call it honesty. It feels like we must set things straight about the nature of reality, while at the same time realizing our own infinite power of creating it. If I honestly choose to see my state of awareness clearly, something in me will always know. Calling it intuition, awareness or soul doesn't change anything—it starts with plain honesty.

Another powerful aspect of honesty is to catch myself when I use my meditation for my "personal gain" instead of a deeper spiritual purpose. And maybe there isn't such a huge difference between the two. What I'm saying here is that God doesn't judge what we do. For me, this kind of honesty can be described as a singular point where the eternal Spirit and my tiny self keep coming together and drifting apart.

This honesty—which I sometimes also call *sobriety*—defines who I am and what my *purpose* is here. It's an ongoing, never-ending moment of the creation of my intentional individual existence within all there is. This honesty is all that I really have in terms of a soul-compass to guide my journey on the path of spirituality. If I ever wanted to know myself, this is how.

Just one moment of being in that honesty is enough. Just arriving there is already an awakening, or as I call it, a quantum enlightenment, one of a countless number to be experienced in a single lifetime.

I use technology to set an alarm several times a day to practice my one-minute meditation, also called *quantum breath* by James Mahu, to whom I am profoundly grateful for his infinite inspiration. Wherever I am and no matter what I find myself involved in when the alarm goes off, I shift gears and commence meditating instantly. More often than not, I can reach my place of honesty, thus rejuvenating my sense of being alive, while training my awakening in a sustained manner, lessening the control of the mind and illusion in my life.

It is easy.

"Truth is only a feeling of heartfelt honesty."
—Ink by Star, Book 21: *Pegasus*

WHAT IS DEATH?

Throughout my life, countless times, I've entered a state of complete, mindless panic brought about by the sheer terror of dying. Every time, it was the same. It never lessened in intensity or significance. It remained a constant for me, always lying dormant, an eternal threat hanging above my head to this very day, and striking a devastating blow each time I fully experienced it. Or perhaps I should say, to the day I had another grand revelation, about sixteen years ago.

"Our fear of dying is actually our false self's terror of the imminent awakening."
—Ink by Star, Book 5: *Lyra*

No control

The day was fine for a soccer match. As long as it was dry, that was all that mattered to me. Rain and wet grass made the ball so much harder to control. For too long, I'd been toiling to learn the ropes of this sport. After finally reaching a level where I could honestly say I was satisfied with my play, I wasn't eager to let the external circumstances diminish my skill. But somehow it seemed to me that there was always something after me, trying to sabotage my aspirations of being great at something.

One of the perennial problems with our amateur friends and family soccer matches was that it was awfully hard to gather enough people for two teams. I was even used to playing one on one, and three against two was usually the norm. Regardless, I loved soccer and would go far out of my way to get players together. That day, the attendance was extraordinary. As it happened, some other enthusiasts were playing on the field when we arrived, and we merged with them, forming two strong teams of six.

Since I'd started dating my girlfriend—whom I already wrote about in an earlier chapter—I didn't care that much about the quantity of players, coming to realize that quality was enough. As a professional sports player and a passionate sportswoman in general, she raised the bar for all of us in terms of ambition and dedication to our every move, pass, and shot. Our stamina was good—we were known to play matches for two or even three hours straight, in all weather and any season. We loved and lived soccer.

My deepest desire at that time was to score a perfect goal with the assistance of my girlfriend. As I always insisted we play on the same team, there were certainly opportunities for that. But just like in professional, big-screen soccer matches, well, things went wrong too. I had to wait for quite some time before I got my wish.

When she volunteered—as she usually did—for the corner kick, I couldn't say I was ready. But there I was and the ball flew directly to me. It was a high one and I sprung up in the air as powerfully as I could, reaching far above the two heads of the defense, peaking at the perfect moment, hitting the ball and sending it straight into the goal's top-right corner.

Score!

It was a moment of success and sheer celebration that I let myself enjoy more than ever before. Pure joy mixed with a sense of achievement and pride, but mostly it was love and the feeling of having accomplished something together as true partners. My girlfriend and I ran towards each other, falling into a spectacular embrace. I could see heads turning our way with smiles of approval. Everyone was happy for us.

Just a week later my perfect world cracked as she told me her ex-boyfriend had contacted her and she needed some time for herself. I had been acutely aware of her unfinished story with him, yet I was clinging to the hope that our new story would overwrite theirs. But it wasn't that easy and I knew I might not get to be that lucky. She wanted us to remain friends and still play soccer together until she figured out what she wanted, and I was okay with that.

The next match was different though.

Heavy, dark clouds hovered ominously above the field. Uncertainty lingered in the air. I'd have much preferred that either the rain poured or the sun shone, so we could have at least known where we stood. But c'est la vie.

Of course, I was troubled by more than the lousy weather or the number of players, which was low. My heart was hurt, if not broken. I loved her and I felt how great we could be together... But she had other options open now.

She played for the other team that day. Even when she wasn't on the ball, I repeatedly snuck glances at her, wondering if I could do anything to save our relationship. How could I win her once and for all? I knew I wasn't a completely ordinary or normal guy in the broad sense of the words. But that was good, wasn't it? I was good. At least I believed I was. Was I not good enough for her? Better than... others? Would she indeed leave me?

Keeping score was never my strength and on that day I had no idea whether we were winning or losing. Instead of focusing on the game, I observed the dreary sky, and the scents of summer grass freshly mowed on the adjacent field stirred my emotions.

I was sad, but that was not all.

I was afraid too.

Scared of loss. Scared of the loss of my love.

Looking straight at her diagonally across the playing field, I saw her as she was: a complete, independent, and powerful being, capable of making her own choices and following her own path.

A deep shiver ran down my spine.

And I knew then: she was already gone.

Her choice had been made, even if she wasn't aware of it yet herself. She was leaving me and that was final.

I sobbed involuntarily and felt dizzy.

Time stopped.

Nobody had broken my heart before.

An enormous feeling enveloped me like an ocean of thick darkness.

It was larger than life. I felt helpless, completely and utterly powerless to affect the outcome of this most important situation I was facing. It was absolutely beyond my control. I was certain without a doubt that there was not one single word I could say or thing I could do to shift what was unfolding and what was going to happen. I had no way of changing her mind or affecting her decisions at all.

I was petrified.

My heartbeat accelerated from more than my exertion of running. I was terrified of not knowing what would happen to me and of not having a say in it. I hated this. The feeling of not wanting to be in this situation was nearly impossible to bear. My whole body was shaking and I felt like I was standing on the edge of a precipice, on the verge of a nervous breakdown. I had to break free.

But how?

I felt an urge to seek and find someone—anyone really—who would restore my sense of reality, my trust that everything was alright. Then I realized that I had felt the same way before: whenever I sensed the threat of my inevitable death!

Wow.

But this time it felt different. For the first time in my life, I could clearly discern between my feelings of anticipating death and the feral fear of my utter lack of control.

Being dead is not scary.

Having no say about it, is.

The magnitude of my realization was such that it blew away all my thoughts and feelings. My mood cascaded into one of wonderment.

I was in awe.

This state lasted for a few seconds. Then the ball flew from nowhere and hit me in the back of my head, returning me to the world of the living.

I looked at my girlfriend and she smiled at me.

I smiled back.

It was okay.

I would be okay, either way.

But what *is* death?

I don't really know. What is it to you? Do you feel anything when you think about death?

Is the question "what is death?" being answered with intuition about what we may experience after we die? I don't believe we can really intuit that. Whatever I can intuit, I also intuit that there is a great chance the mind is adding too much of that virtual veneer that makes everything seem real, even though it's not.

The furthest I dare to go when speculating about death is to take my experience of stopping the world and imagine it to last forever: to exist with absolutely no mind. Yet considering that we not only live in the mind, but also in the body, I'd say that these filters alone would skew any intuitions about death more than we can tell.

However, when posing the big question about what death is, I mean something else entirely. I simply mean: how do you feel *now* when you become aware of your unavoidable death? Do you have any sensations or emotions about it?

My reaction to attuning my focus on death is the one I described above and in an earlier chapter: the terror of losing absolutely all control. Maybe that is not everyone's response. Perhaps it's just some of my biggest traumas and dramas manifesting. What about you? What is your emotional response?

There is a viable benefit to paying attention to death: the clear, honest awareness of the utter non-importance of everything transient, which is, well, everything in the world.

Again, not that nothing matters—but that everything matters equally.

When I manage to arrive at that jolt or shock, it does feel terrifying at first, but then it renders my present situation, whatever it is—smooth and manageable. Lovable. Because I love life. I love living and experiencing. It's hard to admit, but yes: even the difficult parts, even the toil and suffering. I abhor the thought of losing that altogether and forever.

As soon as I stop clinging to my life and this world—in other words, to everything that was never even mine—I feel free, light as a feather, limitless. A powerful energy fills me that makes me believe I can do *anything* and actually makes me want to do *everything*—while I still have the chance.

All the little fears become insignificant. For example, when I am facing death, who cares what others think of me? What do I have to lose? In fact, I have so much to gain: all of those tiny, fragile moments that would have been unlived without this awareness!

There is such amazing beauty, so much enchanted mystery everywhere—this everyday churn is larger than life and sweeter than heaven. And it's right there for my taking. And giving. And giving! I have so much to express.

Looking from that grand perspective, my priorities are reset. I am aware of my purpose—even if I don't fully understand it yet in the mind—I sense my fulfillment awaiting me patiently. And still there is no time to lose. Procrastination is just fear of not being enough, but the awareness of my inevitable dying overrides that. All that is left is for me to live, fully, daringly, caringly, having fun, and cherishing the moment.

Live your life as if it were a dream, because maybe it is.

In the words of Carlos Castaneda's teacher and nagual don Juan: *use your death as an advisor*. To me, that is something completely outside of the mind. It is only when I become aware of my own mortality and feel icy death breathing down my neck that I can be fully alive.

The moment I truly grasp *death*, I sense that no matter how big and all-encompassing life seems, death will always be larger. All the concepts in the mind, all the stories and really everything I know and am—all of that is without any meaning in the face of death. When I reach that awareness, I feel as if something utterly, infinitely transcendental, fantastic, and unknowable is out there on a cosmic scale, yet we are all completely oblivious to it.

That sensation shows me with ice-crystal clarity how insignificant my whole being is, relative to my eternal potential, one that I know next to nothing about. It tells me that I am still only starting to learn and grow, and what I have accumulated so far in this lifetime and am clinging to so ferociously is like a child's toy in comparison to the real thing. It tells me that I just shouldn't take everything for granted—nor take myself so seriously.

At the moment when I become acutely aware of death and of my inevitable dying, nothing else remains but awareness. The mind shrinks to zero, and I intuit directly the true discernment between mind and awareness.

It is only when the mind is gone that we can see what it is and who we are.

"Our ultimate fear is not of dying, but of losing our mind."
—Ink by Star, Book 21: *Pegasus*

Grounding

My bare feet stand firmly planted on the dewy autumn grass in my home backyard. Eyes closed, I feel the morning air caressing my skin. I hear birds chirping away and crows flapping their wings, flying over my head to the rooftops. My neighbor starts their car and the engine purrs, then roars, as they drive down the street. Insects are awakening and buzzing all around. I smell damp, nurturing soil and the vegetation—so alive!

I open my eyes. I am standing directly in front of a ten foot tall cypress hedge. Each individual tree exudes its green energy, glistening softly. A thin, barely perceptible fog descends and twirls gently as if dancing with the world. My gaze connects with the distant clouds and at that instant, a crack reveals a portion of the sun and a beam of light brightens the day.

Shivering, I know: I'm dying. Death is inevitable, certain. It's just a matter of time, and all this, my whole life, will be over and gone. Nothing can stop or prevent this. No denial can keep covering it up forever: there *will* come a time when another crack will open and the unknowable will enshroud my being and turn my everything upside down and inside out. The moment of truth. What next? Nobody knows.

All of this, right now, my fears, my heartbeat, my loved and dear ones, the toil, the sweat, the breadcrumbs, the fire in the eyes and the spark in the sinews: where will all that end up?

Will it still mean anything or have importance and significance?

Does it now?

I turn on my heels and walk back into my house. My priorities have shifted.

My time is limited. But the inspiration, faith, and love that I can create, is not.

"Grounding is focusing on something that exists outside of your mind."
—Ink by Star, Book 21: *Pegasus*

MISCREATION

This chapter is perhaps the toughest to write—and read? This is, again, because it's circular. The very subject of what we are discussing here is aware of us observing it, as if we are shining a bright light on a shadowy being existing in the pitch black.

But if we can relax a notch and just be a little funny here, or loony, somewhat carefree, that might help break the ice. Have faith, as I do, that it's not all bad—nothing is. So let's smile and enjoy the ride.

Perhaps we could also take a deep breath right here.

...

Now let's refocus again, as primal explorers: what are we doing at this point? What do we want again?

I want to break free. Yes, I want to release a control in the mind, the submind, that—as I've come to learn through decades of conscious experience—does incredible things to my cognition and perception, to the point that it's hard to be sure of what is real and what is an illusion. It is even nearly impossible to know who I am at all.

That last point is exactly why "know thyself" lies at the core of all wisdom. It was never about mental understanding, but about awakening awareness. Sustained primal exploration reveals that the question of who we are may start with who we are *not*.

First off, we are not crazy. That is actually something quite important to consider. As soon as the intelligence of awareness is present, we know without a doubt that we are sane and sober, though we realize we may all be living in a spooky upside-down world, in a manner of speaking. But honestly, that's just how a part of ourselves views the world. There's so much confusion. Consider: the world *is* perfect as it is. And so are you.

Are you aware of your many facets? Of being split within?

You see, there's this dualism, or even pluralism, that causes an inner strife. Very rarely are we at complete peace with ourselves, or with the world for that matter—which is weirdly related, isn't it? As within, so without...

What if to some degree we *all* are schizophrenic, every last one of us? How do *you* perceive yourself? Do you always clearly and singularly know what you want? Or do you ever feel you are a bit confused, conflicted, and even contradicting yourself internally?

Furthermore, do you ever notice how much you can shift, not just your emotions and your mood—but more than that, to the point where at times it may seem to you as if you become a completely different person? For example, you may feel like you've become someone else entirely if something triggers you and you react against your best judgment, and say or do something really bad you regret a minute later, or the next day.

Where is that aggression, all that negativity, and the seemingly evil disposition coming from? You know you are really not like that. Why would you ever turn into something so opposed to who you are, even if only temporarily and against your desire?

Could these dark shifts we experience be the main reason that we end up judging ourselves and stop trusting and loving ourselves? We fight against ourselves and that is hard. It makes us feel that there is something intrinsically wrong with us and maybe the whole world.

We begin to see life as suffering. We keep saying to ourselves that we are not worthy, sufficient, or complete.

Of course, those are extremes and I am only speaking from my own experience. I sometimes think and feel that way, but I would never presume you or anybody else does. Still, if you experience a hint of the above havoc even on a minuscule level, it could prove beneficial if we can manage to see through this internal schism with more clarity and honesty. It may turn out that most of us here at this time suffer daily from the unwanted tiny shifts and negative transformations we undergo when we get affected by certain triggers that we may or may not understand at all.

It's curious that we don't talk about this openly and systematically. Why are we demonizing this condition of being split within? Why do we insist on believing there exists only a minor percentage of people with such inner conflict and other psychological conditions—which are often treated as diseases?

The answers are simple. It's all circular, again, and we must wait to see the complete picture. As above, so below. As the individual, so the whole society. What if this is indeed an unprecedented mystery that humanity has only now started to unravel?

Keenly listening to all of my intuition, I can't stress this enough: this issue is huge! It is the foundation of all that is causing problems and suffering in the world, and it begins when we argue and fight over our truths.

But how can decent human beings be part of the problem? It is because we are not fully aware that we are.

For as long as we stick to enacting a role of who we think we are, and clinging to our beliefs and values all the while, we are doomed.

There's nothing wrong with our role, or anybody else's. We are all striving to be good. Yet our good intentions and beliefs are nevertheless paving the way to hell instead of heaven, for some uncanny reason. Why is that so?

You can ask that of your own intuition. Be soft around knowing the answer. It may be misleading.

The way I see it, each of us is internally divided. Energetically, we contain many separate beings within ourselves. Sounds preposterous, doesn't it?

I write of miscreation in the chapter about breathwork, because that is where we can see it the most clearly. At some point in our lifetime, during a fateful and extreme—usually negative—event, even if only as a coping mechanism, we created an alternative "I" and we started to feed it energy on a regular basis by believing that we *are* it. Every time a similar event or circumstance repeated, we relived the original event and added even more of our precious belief onto the fire of miscreating. After a time of sustaining this, the new self adopted a life of its own, within our own being, not unlike a parasite.

Now, some say the source energy of this parasite is external, that it comes from elsewhere, that it's inhuman or even alien. Some call it an *entity*, or a *flyer*, and some name it a *pain body*. That may all be true, or none of it may be. I strongly feel that at this point, as we are reading and writing this, it's not productive to focus on what this miscreation actually is.

Instead, let's explore how it affects us and what we can do about it!

To refocus: our perennial confusion stems from our internal division. There are two or several practically independent personalities in us, constantly balancing or canceling each other out.

Would you like to take your time here and observe if there is anything like that within you too? Perhaps take a gentle, deep breath first.

...

Can you possibly witness how you are split into many parts?

Now, super-slowly ask yourself, intuitively, as the primal explorer you are:

Which of these personas are you? Are you able to choose them?

Does either of the above change through time?

Are you, perchance, all of them at once?

Are you aware of the other personas when you are being one of them?

And what about right now—who are you at this moment?

Where are the other ones now? Who are they really?

We have all likely had a lot of experience with living as the different personas within us. But to the mind, it may all appear hazy and hard to think about. That is the denial in action, as the submind silences our true mind and overrides any intuition we may have.

Remember all those episodes in your life when you argued with somebody about something? When you felt so right and so righteous? When you perhaps felt threatened by another's viewpoint? Misunderstood? Not heard? Maybe you didn't feel worthy? Not good enough? Were there times when you wanted to do something good, but you just couldn't start? When you procrastinated? Or when you did something bad, but you couldn't own it and accept the consequences, or you simply couldn't apologize? When you knew you should be honest and admit your fault, but couldn't bring yourself to do it, because it would have made you appear and feel weak?

We are not merely waging wars with other people or our loved ones—we are desperately and mercilessly battling ourselves.

We can be our own worst enemy.

Until we are not! Until we learn self-love.

We are the ones who torture ourselves, go against our greatest good, and make ourselves miserable. By doing so we become so sour, sore, and eventually so insensitive that our actions, words, and thoughts appear evil. If we are being brutally honest: we cause conflicts too, we take sides, we fight for freedom against anybody of different color or creed, and so on and so forth—we all know that part. But that is just one side of the coin, the outward appearance, the tip of the iceberg—which always starts with inner division and the miscreations of diminished awareness.

Again, I want to refocus, start fresh, and let go of anything fixating my attention too much. Doing that as often and as honestly as it takes may be the best way to support and train our awareness awakening.

So I ask myself at this point: what do I really want, in the long run?

I want to stop feeling and acting as if I am my own mortal enemy!

I also want to be happy, strong, and move forward, singing along the way. My scorching desire is to finally cease sabotaging myself. I just want to live peacefully, in harmony with nature. I want to enjoy my days, my family and friends, and my work, my creation.

I want this lifetime to count. I want to express my uniqueness and be a present for the world. I want to move mountains, and people, and leave a sacred mark here.

Do I have to ever fully understand what is standing in my way—inside—in the mind and the nervous system?

No. Not understand, because that avenue is closed to us for the time being: it is usurped and hijacked by the miscreation. Understanding is not possible now, but luckily, it's also not necessary.

This whole book is geared towards circumventing the need to understand, and yet somehow inspiring us to grok all that is going on in our lives. We know that by now.

So what would a primal explorer do?

For as long as the submind is in complete control, there is no realizing where the ultimate agenda is coming from. The miscreated, parasitic and abusive energy will somehow—working through the mind—always find a way to come off as: love!

Can you believe that? That is how it gets us! Or should I say: that is how I get myself, because that is what is happening. Focusing on this as if there was an external enemy—or in fact an enemy of any kind—is merely more fuel for the miscreated energies, making them stronger.

Why is that? If we manage to quiet down the submind enough to hear and trust our intuition, we can observe the whole process over time. We can witness firsthand that whenever we think, speak, or act from an agitated, polarized mind, the outcome will invariably contain an underlying subterfuge with a singular goal: to keep the dualistic submind in charge! The miscreation convinces us to even further shroud ourselves from awareness in this self-destructive way with a delayed payment. Yes, we live on fake credit. For all the false love and immediate gratification the miscreations will entice us with, we'll have to settle the bill in the form of our suffering down the road, as sure as death (but not taxes). My humor again…

So what is there to do? What *can* we possibly do, forever trapped in such an impossible and untenable situation? If it is indeed circular, how can we ever hope to free ourselves from the vicious cycle?

There is a way out, I promise you!

The first step is believing that a first step exists. It entails faith—mindless, blind faith, yes, but perfectly grounded and profoundly steeped in the core of our true being and our cosmic awareness. We have been practicing this all along. I feel that you have likely prepared yourself thoroughly for this, or you wouldn't be reading these words now. We are all seasoned, ever-awakening, heartful co-creators of what is to come.

I have said it before and I will keep saying this always: the way through is here in our heart and in our body, in our blood and sweat, in our organic life interconnected with nature and elements, stars, and love! Most specifically: the way through is *not* in the mind alone.

Ancient cultures all lived outside of the mind's control. Even in more recent times, their techniques lead them to vanquish the submind and remove it from the driver's seat, over and over again, if need be. They have remained aware of the significance of awareness, and also of what is *not* awareness.

In order to transcend the confusion constantly upheld by the miscreation working through the mind, we must outcreate it! I am borrowing the word *outcreate* from my dear friend and teacher David Elliott, as he has already imbued it with so much self-love and awareness that it is truly special now, indeed, it is specialized!

There is no way to explain what outcreation is. It's best that we just use it, just do it. Our spirit knows how. Follow its lead and have faith. Intend it.

We will outcreate the need for distraction whenever we don't feel we are enough.

We will outcreate the fear of having to show up and commit to this life.

We will outcreate the worry and hardship of taking care of all that we love—which seems to seep through our fingers every now and then.

We will outcreate the sadness of being a human being, believing our angelic wings have been clipped off by the ones we have trusted the most—and by love itself.

We will outcreate the rage and frustration of being misunderstood, of all our great intentions backfiring, and suffocating in the confines of the golden cage we call the mind.

We will outcreate the pretense, the lie of false promises, the trickery of goodness slaughtering evil and everything that is different and strange.

We will outcreate ourselves and each other by reaching for the loving form we can adopt for the occasion of awakening from a slumber deeper than death.

We will outcreate the miscreation.

"You can't outsmart your mind but you can outcreate it."
—Ink by Star, Book 22: *Ursa Minor*

Human Form

Let us both ground this somewhat elusive chapter with a deep breath full of sweet consciousness right at the beginning.

...

Going back to the invaluable question of *who am I?* as primal explorers, let's now reflect on how powerfully the miscreations affect the way we see ourselves. For sure, the power is all ours—the miscreation energy has no power itself. And yet, through the constant control and subtle manipulation of the submind's non-stop repeating loops whispering into our inner ear, making it ever harder for us to discern between the miscreation and our true self, we ultimately get so confused, that of our own free will we unwittingly lend all of our power to the intentions of the miscreation.

The breathwork, or any other tool that quiets down the submind, helps us unmask the energy of miscreation to recognize it as it truly is: *not* love—even though it will continuously attempt to convince us that it loves us and wants to protect us, while doing exactly the opposite. Temporarily free from the mind's total control, we can also see who we truly are more clearly, outside of the particular miscreation that we successfully identified.

And, like always, there is more to it.

We may, and usually do, host more than just one miscreation within our energy field, because there may have been many traumatic events in our past or in our family lineage which brought miscreations into existence. These miscreations in effect do cooperate, like seemingly separate, individual heads of one hydra that help each other confuse and polarize us within. We end up fighting ourselves internally, pulled in different directions with contradicting beliefs and convictions that are imposed on and injected into our submind like malignant, hypnotic inceptions.

And still, there is more unknown beneath the surface of our cognition, in regards to who we are. To see a clearer and more complete picture, let's explore the most mysterious viewpoints we can experience in our dreaming states. This will help us grok the human form.

Who are you when you dream? Can you sense the subtle shifts of your perceptions of the world and yourself?

Among many profound dreams I have experienced, I'd like to share one that imbued me with a mysterious, otherworldly feeling. Or perhaps I should say alternative-worldly.

"We are asleep and awake at the same time!"
—Ink by Star, Book 16: *Sagittarius*

A separate reality

I was a prowler in my own home.

It was nighttime, and I couldn't sleep. Instead, I was strolling through the halls of my old house, the house where I used to live when I was a child, the house with all the big memories of my little traumas...

I was aware that I was dreaming.

I checked my hands, routinely. Yep, still there. Not many wrinkles either, and that was good. That meant I was doing great. I was clean and healthy.

I walked on, admiring the walls and the pictures and artwork on them.

This time, as I dreamt, something felt different.

Strangely different.

My dream was more lucid than ever before, and my intent was much more abstract than usual. Instead of wanting to fly around and experience all sorts of fantastic things that I ordinarily couldn't experience outside of dreaming, I simply wanted to learn more about myself, about who I truly was.

A subtle scent in the air stirred my attention. Something was reeking of deep mystery.

I was myself—and at the same time, I was not.

The house with its square, wood-floored rooms and the long, blue-linoleum covered corridor were exactly the same as I remembered them, but then again—not the same at all. I couldn't really say how or why, but I knew there were dimensions to this dreaming reality that I had never before experienced.

Gliding on, disinterested in anything worldly, I wished to follow this feeling leading me towards *who I am*, and savor it through and through.

Who am I?

I felt that I was not just myself, and I was definitely not in my normal world, even for a dream. A weird portal was opening—had already opened—and an awareness of another kind was pouring in. I was being rushed by its flow, carried away, perturbed, peacefully and pleasantly.

The ambient light was otherworldly. It was faint, but that didn't scare me. The twilight was invigorating, empowering. There was a fair brown hue permeating every nuance of my attention. A chestnut tinge. I could smell it.

The scenery reminded me of a nostalgic music video with a heavily distorted color palette and daring filters, but sans music. Just the nurturing silence of a thick night.

My footsteps echoed softly. Barefoot, I felt the floor under my feather weight. The slight cold was not uncomfortable. Nothing in that dream felt wrong or bad. If anything, it was the antithesis of a nightmare.

I smiled to myself, happy that my dreaming attention was still holding. There seemed to be no hurry, not that time. I must have been on a special time. God's time, or something like that. I was connected. To what exactly, I did not know...

When it seemed that my experience just couldn't get more surreal, I noticed a mirror hanging on the living room wall.

Now, *this* was different! In the house of my waking life, there was no mirror there. Yet there was one here now, and I was both anxious and curious to see myself in it.

I approached and peered in.

A man in his fifties or perhaps sixties was staring at me. His face was still and stern, a solemn mask. His receding hairline looked almost pathetic, but who was I to judge him, knowing well that he *was* me, in some fantastic sort of twisted interconnectedness.

He appeared sad, but not depressed. Maybe a bit worn out and bored with his life. A little trapped. Alone, perhaps. Not around kids enough, I guessed. Did he have a life? A real life? Yes, he did. I had no doubt about that. His profession must have been on the slow side.

He could have been an undertaker or a mortician; that was the vibe I was getting.

The man kept gazing at me, and I realized his reality was just as real as mine.

He was also probably dreaming his own dream right now, maybe walking through his own home, and wanting to check on himself in the mirror—bam!—he had encountered me instead of his face. Likewise, it hadn't scared, disgusted, or deterred him in any way; it hadn't caused him to stop looking and move away.

An ancient curiosity was written all over his face, woven in the wrinkles of his skin.

His brown eyes were so dissimilar to my blue green eyes, and yet... and yet... They were mine.

I didn't feel this stranger was me; I *knew* he was.

There was a connection here, transcending everything.

We *were* this connection, and we were spanning a bridge across forever, he and I. Just about everything in between was formed by our awareness, beyond our own understanding or concern.

We took one last glance at each other, with enough intensity to fill a lifetime, and then I moved on without a second thought, and so did he, I knew, in his own world, which was weirdly, also my own.

My sense of this split reality was growing stronger by the minute. But it was not a split as in a rift. There was nothing broken, there was no abyss or crevice to surmount or heal or merge back together. The split had the nature of expansion, or perhaps of a computer copy/paste operation, where one thing becomes two, and potentially more. Some kind of universal cloning on the highest and deepest level.

My awareness was now forever tainted with knowing that another me existed in some far-away dimension, and that we were and had always been, one.

I was an apple being eaten by the snake of duality, and there was no going back to the paradise of oblivion.

And even though it was challenging, I sensed that I *was* in paradise as well, a paradise of knowing.

Yes. It was all good now. Couldn't be any other way…

I walked to the balcony door, opened it, and stepped outside.

I saw the sky. It was daytime.

The cars on the street all looked the same. Everything felt so familiar. It was like returning to the seventies—maybe more like the eighteen seventies, not nineteen—with a strong hint of something even more fantastic, out of a fairy tale or a comic book I may have once read.

Like in the times of my youth, there was this benevolent and happy feeling of abundance, of everyone having enough. The socialist regime of my childhood, no matter how criticized, had been great indeed. And this dream, even more so. Everything seemed to be commonly shared and equal, uniform: all the cars driving by were the exact same model.

I strained my eyes to read the model name on a car. It simply said *gogo*. They were all gogo cars!

For some reason, this made me unbelievably happy!

In that world, everybody drove these simple plain cars that looked a little like the old Beetle, but smaller, and they were all more or less the same light lime color, with red childish letters saying gogo on them.

Here, life felt infinitely simple, lending me the incredible feeling of inherent safety. It was like the whole world was my playground once again, and life was a funny, joyful game.

Reaching the end of the balcony, I turned a corner. Some construction workers were renovating the neighbor's house facade. They worked steadily and with gusto. They loved their job, I could tell. It seemed as if they, too, were playing a game.

Everything still felt so strange, albeit in a good way…

What did I expect? I was dreaming, after all!

The house of the next neighbor then attracted my attention and I was being pulled towards it strongly.

I started to levitate and float and I flew towards that house.
I woke up before I touched it.

This dream opened something profound in me that I had never experienced before and is impossible for me to describe. The mysterious shift I sensed was not directly related to any of the dream elements, but rather to my sentiments and especially my overall awareness. In the way that the next story below is connected to what I believe the human form is, in a subtle yet meaningful way, the dream was related to the question of *who am I*?

But before connecting all the dots, let's collect some more viewpoints first.

One key viewpoint to consider is what I call a subtle loss of consciousness.

When we've been training awakening for some time, even that becomes a routine. It's normal that repetitive tasks are delegated to the subconscious. Even driving, in all its complexity and importance because of the safety risks, is something we're doing on autopilot.

We pursue the goal of awakening for so long that we tend to normalize that sentiment. Moreover, we may reach a phase that whenever we meditate, we just go through the motions, but our soul and awareness are not there. We *think* we meditate as we sit in silence, and we *think* the mind is quieting down and our internal dialog is gone, but it's not. Instead, we are telling ourselves a story of how we are meditating and shutting down the mind and how we are awakening. We are engaged in a dialog about us doing this, rather than us actually doing it. It's not real—it's just like a dream.

So how can we tell whether we actually do meditate and awaken?

When the Spirit is moving and your consciousness awakens, you always know without a single doubt. You are not in the domain of the mind any longer, where results can be measured and therefore trusted. Soul science is different. The honesty and trustworthiness of experience is guaranteed by our grounding and sobriety, or clarity.

Becoming conscious of being alive is a process that is neither linear nor dual. We can use our present awareness of who we are to imbue our memories with this living awareness, until we believe that our consciousness has been there, in our past experiences, from the start. As we do this every day and every moment, these experiences become more than merely memories, reveries, or fantasies. We are making them all real, as if traveling through time. By doing this, we overwrite our memories and in a sense, change both what happened in the past and who we were.

This life is a dream in many ways. One of the dream aspects is the way the mind upholds the illusion of reality. It does this by building filters into our cognition. The mind starts with our perception, and the underlying sensorial stimuli, but then adds countless interpretations from the complex mesh of our past traumas, inherited patterns of beliefs, and cultural programs. The mind can obscure absolutely everything if we have no viewpoint completely independent of the mind. The only element in existence that is truly outside of the mind's control, is awareness. You can call it Spirit, or Nagual. The less you call it, the better.

When we sense an awakening within and we believe our awareness has increased or was somehow enhanced, what we're in fact experiencing is simply the mind quieting down and thus partially releasing its usual control over our cognition. The more the mind relaxes, lets go, quiets down, pauses, or even steps away entirely, the more aware we are. There are no actual degrees of awareness, or levels of being awake—there are only openings within the mind's operation. We can train ourselves daily to help these occur more frequently, for longer periods of time, and more thoroughly.

However, as we train our awakening, the mind will always catch up with it a little later and notice what we're doing. The mind—or we should we be clear about it and say *the miscreation with the submind*—will do absolutely anything to preserve its role on top of the food chain, and so the miscreation will start figuring out that our practice of awakening is truly a dangerous thing, for not only its dominance, but for its existence, and it will do its best to stop it.

We can become distracted, feel unworthy and just plain tired, or we can become super certain that we've already arrived and that we need no further practice whatsoever. Sometimes, we can simply forget entirely about our daily practice and it will take days before we even realize we've stopped doing it, without knowing why.

But one thing is sure: it's the submind and the miscreation in the background that is doing this. It will always succeed at first in convincing us that it is trying to protect us, and that its gifts are love, joy, and peace. Yet as you will invariably discover: it is quite the opposite. This is how the miscreation works: it lies and manipulates in order to survive. It may sound simple in theory, but in practice it takes all the awakened awareness we can summon to catch a clear glimpse through the fog of its subtle deception. Yep, again: it's circular.

That moment when we feel the hardest pull to stop our practice—for whatever reason—is *key*! That is where our one cubic centimeter of chance lies.

Seize it!

Do you really know what is at stake here?!

Does anyone completely understand what it signifies to lose consciousness and to exist only on autopilot? Is it not obvious that our absolute top-priority should be to keep training our awakening, even more than we do anything else in our everyday life?

Meditate daily, and see through and seize such key moments of becoming aware of losing consciousness—that's all.

One essential approach to awakening in this very moment is this: pause to witness everything out there as *one*—not only the objects, but also the space and the energy field you're in; not only the beings around you, but also your relationship with them and your feel-ings—your exchange with it all! Experience the oneness.

And just have faith and keep up the good work.

That's all any of us can ever do.

Let me tell you another story that helped me look at this from yet another angle. We'll integrate it all by the end of the chapter, at least in the soul syntax, if not with the mind, I promise.

When I was thirty-five, I attended another of Carlos Castane-da's workshops in Barcelona with a group of great friends, and I experienced something so subtly powerful and meaningful to me on a level I couldn't possibly understand, that it was second only to my "stopping the world" experience.

There is a concept that don Juan talks about in Castaneda's books, called the *human form*.

When the shamans of ancient Mexico perceived energy as it flowed through the Universe, before it was interpreted by the mind, they could *see* a human being as a luminous blob, a field of bright light with a precise boundary in the shape of an egg.

They witnessed that the internal flow of energy, which they perceived as countless shiny filaments, tended to stop in many segments, as if blocked, instead of vigorously circulating. This stagnant energy would gradually become deposited on the sides of the egg, forming a crust that dulled the overall glow of the human being, thus diminishing our fluidity of perception and awareness.

My own intuition tells me how a miscreation solidifies as a sticky block within our energy field and how through the whis-perings of the submind, it establishes and maintains a permanent control of most, if not all, of our perceptions and interpretations.

The consistent practice of awakening, using any kind of med-itation, will open the blocked energy centers and restore the flow of awareness.

At this point, I invite you once more to draw a deep, juicy breath, and savor it in your body for a prolonged moment. Perhaps you will even sense an inner smile blossoming in your heart, informing you that all is well.

...

Now let's return again to the billion dollar question of who we are.

As primal explorers, we trust our intuition and we completely grok the play of our awareness as a vibration coursing through our physical being. Its free flow results in the clear perception of whatever we focus on. Any blocks will skew the interpretations and bring about layers of delusion and rigid, false beliefs.

You can see yourself as an angel or a devil, as powerful or weak, invaluable or worthless, eternal or lost. You can believe you are a Spirit-shard wearing a human suit, or a flesh-and-blood thinking machine imagining yourself to be a god. Or even all of the above at once.

But what remains beyond the many identifications that we can choose from?

Is there anything real, specific, and constant that truly defines us? What makes us human for as long as we're alive in this body—and more importantly: what makes us the kind of human we are?

Who am I, as this individual walking though my life today?

According to Carlos Castaneda, and also my experience, yes: there is something that defines us ultimately and completely within the scope of our lifetime. The shamans *saw* the human form as a specific, individuated energy configuration which the Universe consolidates from conscious filaments of infinity at our conception, using the *human mold* as a press.

None of that is something the mind could ever fathom fully, so a mere academic curiosity and a mental analysis of it, is pointless and futile. However, each of us can experience our own human form, prior to any interpretations, firsthand.

The power of such an experience may ground us, shake up our whole life, and open us to new avenues of pursuing our true purpose. In an experience like that, a treasure is hidden: a profound meaning and a sense of fateful fulfillment, pertaining exclusively to ourselves.

Would you like to experience it?

> "You are not the sum total of all your parts but the connecting space between them."
> —Ink by Star, Book 17: *Capricornus*

A safe haven

After many hours of diligently practicing the magical passes, as Carlos Castaneda had named those otherworldly movements resembling both tai chi and martial arts, I had to use the bathroom. Worrying for a moment about what everyone would think of me if I left in the middle of a session, my heart raced hard. I blushed, looking around surreptitiously.

Nobody was watching me directly. I felt relieved.

"I really have to go," I justified myself to myself. "I hope they'll understand..."

Ill at ease, I crept away from my spot, feeling guilty, but pretending that I didn't have a single worry under the sun. I strolled nonchalantly towards the exit of the large, concrete-walled hall, while holding my breath and dying of shame inside.

Two of the Tensegrity (which is another name for magical passes) facilitators were beaming down from the central stage, patiently demonstrating the latest series of passes that had never before been revealed to the public: the Sabretooth Tiger form. Their toned bodies showed how perfectly fit they were, and how happily they were moving around, prancing like tigers and striking with their hands through the air like cobras.

The white neon lights complemented the powerful sunshine coming through the narrow windows that ran up the whole height of the abundant space. Making my way between a mass of two hundred eager, albeit somewhat tired participants, I could smell the distinct scent of healthy sweat: the kind you produce when you are happy, balanced, and unstressed.

Women and men of all sizes, shapes, and ages stood on their colorful yoga mats and paid stern attention to the sequence of movements, trying to repeat them as faithfully as possible. It wasn't easy at all, for the movement units themselves were complex, and a huge number of them were arranged into a dreamfully choreographed succession that was as aesthetically pleasing as it was physically demanding.

Learning those passes demanded one's complete focus, engaging our kinesthetic memory, and as such was enormously taxing to the linear mind—which was one of the key intentions behind it, not unlike meditation.

The other major aspects of the magical passes, which shamans of ancient Mexico had discovered during states of heightened awareness while dreaming awake, were a beneficial, healing redistribution of energy in the human being and an overall improvement of one's mood and well-being. This improvement occurred by adopting certain postures and positions for a prolonged time that proved incredibly beneficial to the body in the long run, bringing about longevity and general health.

Casually and briskly, I pulled the blue metal door open and slid through the bright opening to my personal freedom. I tried to relax while still being careful to silently close the door behind me with just a muffled clack.

The hallway was bathed in the orange, early afternoon sun of a lazy summer Sunday in southern Spain. My heart fluttered. I felt so happy and thankful for being able to join that workshop, and to be in the great, loving company of some of my best friends. There was probably nothing else in the world that I'd rather be doing right then, and nowhere else I'd want to be.

After relieving myself, I walked to the white porcelain sink and opened the cold water to wash my hands and splash some over my face, red from the exertion of the day.

Glancing at the mirror, I saw how green my eyes were. They were normally bluish, with a tinge of brown and green mixed in, but in the ambient luminosity, my strongly contracted pupils made my iris appear shiny, picturesque, and downright magnificent!

I could almost see a reflection of the mirror in the image of my eyes I was staring at in the mirror.

Circular! *What does a mirror reflect in another mirror?*

For a moment, I felt dizzy.

Something opened up in my head.

An emptiness, a complete void entered the room where the mind used to be. My total essence shifted to my heart and whole body instead. I was realizing that it had always been there anyway. Why would I ever even consider that I was *located* in the head?

The water kept running.

I felt the chill porcelain of the sink under my hands, as I grasped for some support and grounding.

The moment was good. I felt exalted and joyful, absolutely present.

I felt *myself*.

The most *myself* I had ever felt in my life.

Gazing at my own, so utterly familiar face in the mirror, I realized I had never seen it before. I had failed to recognize it—like a well-known name one suddenly can't remember. Each pore, every hair, its entire shape and look—all so thoroughly foreign.

Who is this man in the mirror?

Who *am* I?

Who am I, *really*?

Something broke in me.

There was an infinite gap in my consciousness happening right there and then.

The whole reality seemed like it was being redefined or created from scratch.

Immobile, I kept witnessing my eyes and my face, meditatively, as if in a fairy tale or a vivid dream, and the memories of many beings passed through me, all of them being me.

I had arrived, smiling, contemplating being alive.

That was me.

I knew then.

I could see the whole of me, the totality of my being, eternal and fluid, undefined by understanding of any kind. And within it, a proper subset, was the person that I was. A man I had been creating, imagining, defining and redefining over and over again throughout my lifelong collage of experiences, sensations, perceptions, desires, and beliefs...

I witnessed my human form.

Beneath it, and really everywhere in my energy field and my body, in every organ and every cell, I was aware of my soul permeating the *me* that I was trying to know. The soul belonged to something larger, something infinite: the Spirit. But at the same time, the whole of Spirit was also contained within just my soul.

At that moment, in a flash of intuition, I somehow grokked not only the eternal, mysterious interplay between my soul and Spirit, but also *my* relationship with each of them, and both of them together.

There was something that I sensed as my true center, my most focused meaning or my unique purpose for existing, and also the inherent manner of *how* I existed, experienced, and expressed myself.

What I sensed was the "I" that remained even when I stopped identifying with it.

On my countless surfaces, everywhere, both within and without, a veneer had been revealed, layer upon layer of *who I am not*. Some of these living interpretations originated from the miscreations in me, some from the miscreations I inherited from my family lineage, and some from those I simply synced with. I understood there were generic, overarching miscreations connected to whole groups and conglomerates of false identities. These co-created human formations—artificial, integrated beings—belonged to groups such as a human collective living in one geographical area, an entire nation or race, or even the whole of humanity.

All those false personas and identities inside me seemed to be working together, supporting and enabling one another, thus making the illusion appear solid and consistent. Our own incessant internal dialog—mostly filled with arguing, complaints, finger-pointing, diminishing, doubt, and self-effacement, but also exaggerating, fighting for dominion, asserting, pride, and righteousness—was not real. It was always just one fake component mock-fighting another one, utterly polarizing and exhausting, and producing, in the process, the effect of duality, of right and wrong, good and evil.

What shook me the most, however, was the clarity of knowing that the true "I" was a single, coherent, indivisible, irreducible essence, as opposed to a multitude of descriptive adjectives for properties, each of which could define me from one of countless possible viewpoints. No, there was no such thing as a sum of parts, because there were no parts which would compose me into being. Such understanding belonged to the linear mind, and was reinforced daily by the submind.

If we really were a composite of many components, mutually more or less independent, the potential of a split, a schism, or a breaking point would lurk perennially over, and indeed within, our heads. And yes, it most certainly seemed that it did. What we may have feared the most is that we ourselves, in our core, were somewhat miscreated, like a monster, rudely patched together from worn-out spare parts that nobody wanted. We abhorred not being stable, permanent, and constant. We were scared of being inadequate, improper, and insane. We embodied a terrible, on-going inner strife, with paradoxically incompatible pieces of the puzzle that seemed to be clashing and destroying one another with the fury of unresolved hatred.

And yet, none of that was true!

It was merely a well-crafted illusion, however convincing and conniving, spun by the miscreation via the submind, then, now, and forever.

The beautiful man peering through that mirror with his starry, dazzling eyes knew, without a shadow of a doubt, all of that, and more—and together, we were presently grasping my wholeness, my complete invaluable innate worth, my expansive self-love, as well as my predestined free-will mission and lifetime purpose.

It felt cozy and warm, fuzzy, fluffy.

Safe.

Home.

"Your safe space is right in your heart. You carry it within."
—Ink by Star, Book 18: *Aquarius*

SOUL SYNTAX

Why don't we try to *awaken* right now, you and me—what do you say? After all, this is the most important thing to do in our lives.

Can we access a clearer awareness, at this moment?

Can we become more present and attentive to the flow of Spirit?

Can we truly wake up? Wake up from the illusion of—well, everything: of being limited, of being stuck, of believing we know who we are and what we want?

Is it possible to *just do it*, on demand?

We should explore this, primally!

Let's both take a minute here and try it.

...

So what did you do in order to awaken? Are you fully aware of the steps you performed?

May I tell you what I did?

First, I looked around my room and then out of my window. The tree just outside in our yard caught my attention. I could almost smell its green leaves and feel its slender branches and hard bark. I sensed its presence, its patience, its benevolence and generosity. That opened my heart. I felt alive and joyful! I smiled to myself. I slowly closed my eyes and felt into my body, the whole of it. I relaxed deeply. I remembered that I was living a really great life and gratitude poured all over me in waves. For an instant, I was aware of my past and my future—I could witness the gist of my entire lifetime. I knew who I was and what I wanted. My awareness had awakened in some way.

What I just did to awaken is not what I do every time, of course. What I end up doing is a matter of inspiration or instinct. I often do seem to start by looking all around me; only rarely do I close my eyes and focus within, right from the beginning. If there is anything green and alive that I can see outside my window, such as a tree, a shrub, a nice patch of grass, or some plants—even if they are inside, in my room—I'll almost invariably look there first, as if I am drawn to it. My heart will dance with joy when I connect with the deep green color of the chlorophyll—as if I am actually smelling and breathing in some extra-alive oxygen!

My next step—which is quite involuntary, I should add—I'm not following any kind of procedure here—is to let go of my focus and observe everything with my peripheral vision. In a way, I step back, perceptually speaking, to be able to take in more of what surrounds me, and to step out of the way of it. This way, I feel the world becoming more three dimensional in my perception—I can almost sense the higher dimensions unfolding...

After I become aware of the world at large, I start to feel more of myself being part of all that. At the same time, I notice my heartbeat, my breathing, and my bodily feelings and sensations.

Emotions may be present or not. In my case, there may be some elation and a sense of will and presence, a power throbbing through my energy veins. Perhaps I feel like I really want to create something, to bring it into existence. It's a sweet struggle, an effort of concentration, but also a release and letting go—just like in meditation.

Ultimately, I reach a point for which there is no description. True awakening is unfathomable and impossible to talk or even think about. The notions and words we want to use are merely scratching the surface and are oftentimes more misleading than helpful. The act of doing it, the practice itself, is what counts. Over and over again, we can set up the *intent*—and nobody knows what intent is, according to Carlos Castaneda and the shamans of ancient Mexico—to awaken, to be aware, never giving up or losing hope, but trusting the process.

Then I look all around, and let go...

At this point, it happens: the awakening!

Or, it doesn't. It depends on how open I really am, or in other words, how quiet the mind, and specifically, the submind, is.

When you *do* awaken to your soul awareness, you will feel Alive once again, like a child does!

All your pressing and lifelong fears, petty concerns, and underlying unworthiness will vanish without you even trying. A whole new sense of meaning to your life will become apparent. All of your priorities will shift. You will clearly know just how much time and energy you have been wasting every day and how that is not really your fault or responsibility, not with your usual, limited awareness. You will be drawn powerfully and purposefully to the one thing, or maybe more, that you really want to be working on and bringing to fruition and completion in your life in the short time frame available to you before death—and I say that in a honestly hopeful and optimistic tone.

In the state of awareness of being truly awake, your whole cognition will change. Your perception of yourself and of your role in life will not only be different, the very concept of it all will be completely replaced by something that is impossible to describe, not unlike a color that nobody has ever seen. How would you talk about it at all?

Let's just say that each and every meaning in the world will be re-created, and not in the mind, but in your total being. It will be way beyond a mere *Aha!* or *Heureka!* or *Wow!* moment. None of the values of any system we may be familiar with, will matter. This new awareness is what truly lies beyond good and evil, beyond duality, beyond linear understanding. It is ultimately artistic, magical, mystical, and spiritual—and not in any of the old, acquired sense of those meanings.

For practical purposes, this awakened state will open up a brand new avenue, never walked before, towards your true purpose in this lifetime. Not just for you personally—it will imbue you with the compassion of oneness that we often talk about, but which can only ever be honestly experienced in those states of heightened, awakened awareness.

The only key to world peace and synergetic cooperation and energetic exchange among all beings on Mother Earth, in a non-exclusive and sustaining manner, is *this*!

Whether you indeed do awaken or not, or to what degree—in a totally non-linear manner—depends also on countless other factors, of course. Ultimately, the awakening of awareness is entirely out of our control. We get ready; we become willing; we establish our intent—whatever that is—see, what we're doing here is progressing from the linear understanding to the mysterious realm of the unknown, and even touching upon the unknowable.

Be that as it may, my point here is that awakened awareness is not just the *key* element—it is the *only* thing that will ever make a true difference in our lives!

I liken the awakening of awareness in our being with Spirit entering our body and energy field. When the Spirit is moving within us, our life is imbued with a true reality and a deeper purpose, and we can consciously participate in it. We can see more of the larger picture—and especially, we can finally grasp how terribly limited and stuck we normally are, trapped within a singular viewpoint, belief, or pattern that is not even our own.

Claiming that awakening awareness is the only element in our life that will ever make a real difference, is certainly a bold statement, but one I stand behind with all that I am. It is the main reason for the creation of this book.

You see, I believe *this* is what really matters and this, awakening awareness, is where any meaningful and lasting change starts for the healing of our world and humanity itself!

I'm not saying nothing else matters—together, everything adds up, for sure. I'm speaking in terms of our true participation, of *being aware* of what exists and goes on. Awakening awareness can so easily be mistaken for many different levels of engaging with life...

Again, it is like dreaming: when we dream, we may be utterly convinced that the reality we're experiencing is the only reality that exists. No element of the dream—more precisely, no information we obtain in the dream—could possibly open up our awareness to the infinity which lies outside of our limiting dream: not even if we read these exact words in a dream-book, or if a character in our dream told us all about it and went the distance of trying to convince us that we were merely dreaming. Processing information in the mind alone does not affect our awareness directly—neither within a dream, nor outside of it. Mind you, even if we did agree with the premise and actually believed and "knew" that we were dreaming: we still wouldn't truly be *aware* of the difference—our awareness wouldn't be *awakened*—not in the way it would be the very instant we actually wake up from our dream and our sleep. Or, even more powerfully, if we *awakened within* our dream, without waking up.

See the difference?

As we experience such true awakening more often, the mind finds it easier to think about and discuss.

Now, how on Earth can we truly awaken from, or within, *this* dream?

Doing it is what matters, not thinking and talking about it.

Trying is good too, you know, even though some would say "do or do not, there is no try"... But in our book of soul syntax, trying is also doing.

Whatever works for you. As a primal explorer, you can observe all the stagnant beliefs and old rules that may no longer help you, and find and create your own *new* way.

Sometimes I simply look upwards into infinity and recall my mortality. I engage with the awareness of my inevitable death. That delivers a jolt which can help me instantly awaken my awareness. Not every time, but if I can connect with the true *death*, I'm halfway there.

The awakening can also happen quite spontaneously. Without any premeditation or volition on your part, something transcendental just opens you up and makes you experience everything in a different overall mood. I find that it can occur practically under any circumstances. It doesn't matter if my heart is wide open or if I am in the middle of a nightmarish outburst of negativity, immersed in the submind's thought process. To awakening, it's all the same—or so it would seem to me.

My intuition says that we actually can train awakening and thus become more ready to awaken at any moment. We can increase our chances to awaken spontaneously.

One sensation that feels like a close relative of awakening is the good old *déjà vu* we all know. This also just happens by itself, but we can be more or less prepared to be aware of it. If we allow it and leap into its current, it can take us deep and far across the realm of awareness. It tends to dissipate and disappear as soon as the mind kicks in and tries to analyze what is going on.

Another experience we've probably all had is when we try to remember a specific name, such as an actor that we *know* we know. Like in a dream, or with déjà vu, we enter a peculiar, special state of awareness—and let me interrupt myself here: this is *not* a "state of mind," as the phrase goes. In this special state, we instinctively or intuitively just know—everything. We can *see* connections between the actor whose name we can't remember, and movies he was in or people he is associated with. We may distinctly remember events he was part of, such as winning an Oscar, and the emotions we have for him. Just not the name.

Now, what do you do at that point, as you struggle to remember the actor's name? Is there anything you *can* do?

I would like you to now try to return to a memory of one such experience you had, and remember in detail how it feels. What part of you or which components of your being are you attempting to access or use? Are these like some "spiritual muscles" needed to shift something deep within you? I know: wanting to remember that sensation is essentially the same as remembering that actor's name in the first place, isn't it? This too, is circular!

To me, it certainly feels this is body-related, so as I try to remember, I shuffle around, flail my arms, or slowly wave my hands as if in a trance, letting go of the submind's control as much as I can, and entering my primal domain: the sacred body.

Regardless of that process, my most important, long-term approach is definitely daily practice—of whatever that I intuit would help with my awakening—but primarily the breathwork. The key is in doing it as often as needed, but without turning it into yet another routine.

Exercises like remembering obscure feelings or misplaced information are very helpful too. Another one I learned from Carlos Castaneda is to practice always putting on your left sock and shoe first, and then proceeding with the other one. It takes some time before you develop enough—yes, awareness—to even remember you have a task to follow in the first place. With awareness, doing it then becomes easy.

Now consider that after a while of repeating this, it may become a routine for you, and your awareness is no longer involved. It's like driving a car, and other doings we do—they ooze into the subconscious and we're not really present when we do them anymore.

What if that is the story of your whole life? Does everything become a routine? Are we constantly living on autopilot?

That is for you to explore and answer. Who knows—it might be circular...

A similar exercise for the awakening of awareness is when you make a "mental" note to yourself to do something in the future, for example, to take the garbage out. How can you be sure that you won't just forget about it later on? Goodness, has that ever happened to you? I'm just trying to soften the matter with some of my humor again…

So what *do* you do, to actually remember that you have to take out the garbage when the time comes? Or that you have to put the left shoe on first?

Honestly, there is absolutely nothing that we can do about it—except practice and develop our awareness. And not even that. We're not practicing awareness, which is ever-present and infinite. It is just that we have been cut off from it, asleep. We're in fact practicing the *awakening* of awareness. And that gets better as we practice.

Let's ponder, for a moment, the difference between these two practices: remembering to put the left shoe on first, and remembering the name of that actor we forgot. In terms of awareness, if we feel deeply into it, are they not one and the same?

The former demands an awakening that must come out of the blue, without any hints and also without any struggle on our part. The latter, on the contrary, has us work hard and focus at it, because we *want* to remember, and we feel we are almost there and just one more iota of effort is needed—yet we still don't know what exactly we should do to remember that actor's name.

Like the other questions in this book, we'll leave this one unanswered too. We're only interested in the process, the path we're walking here, as we explore the sacred terrain of awareness.

Awareness, and the new soul syntax, are not about answers.

Let's explore further. It may seem that we're engaging mostly the mind when remembering data like a name, but that's not true, is it? We are dealing with kinesthetic memory and probably something deeper and more all-inclusive that we still don't have a word for—or maybe it's just that I don't know about it…

Wanting, aspiring, and toiling to remember what is on the tip of the tongue demands a control that is outside of our conscious reach. But who are we, again? Maybe it's just out of reach for the part of me that is not my whole, and another part of me—or the whole—can easily do it.

Maybe, just maybe, by reaching towards the unreachable goal, I'm also reaching towards my expanded self and actually growing up in new, unprecedented ways. I do believe it's all connected, and circular, yes.

We are not merely awakening—we are creating a fresh awareness in a more expansive and clearly vibrating being, and with it, we are creating a new world—and that is new syntax!

So if you have ever honestly wanted to save the world, to end all wars and suffering, I wholeheartedly invite you to pursue not only your happiness, but also true awakening in your life.

When you do experience the awakening from the everyday dream, you will know, without a doubt. You will recognize it. You may have already been there, many times, but just like awakening, falling back asleep will also happen quite spontaneously and involuntarily—and soon after, the mind will clean up the cognitive "mess" such a true awakening causes to our linear understanding.

We'll keep experiencing these ups and downs until…

Well, until we have practiced awakening for a while, consistently, and have constructed a foundation for it, not only in the mind, but in our hearts. Until we have grounded our curious, inexplicable experience into the deeper reality, growing roots outside of our customary modus operandi, thus extending our whole being with it.

At a certain point, you will reach, if you haven't already, a threshold from which there is no going back, ever. Until the day you die in this human suit, you'll know and remain crystal clear about what true awareness and awakening is.

The end.

Happy ending?

Well, honestly, no. I was kidding. Sorry.

There is no end, no finality to this, to awakening. I don't believe we'll ever be able to reach a plateau of being constantly awake and aware, no matter how popular and coveted this state seems to be these days.

And that, I insist, is good.

To me, it comes and goes in waves and in phases. There are times in my life when I'm more ready to do the work—and it *is* work after all. Every day, a choice has to be made. An intent has to be created for our awakening. We can use many tools, especially meditation—I'll always use breathwork and the one-minute meditation, together with grounding exercises, and some others, of which I write more about in my other books.

I know well that if I don't keep up the good work, which *can be easy*—as my good friend David Elliott keeps telling us—I'll go back to the dark and deep slumber of this era's many distractions and, well, miscreations. I'll lose myself over and over again and will have to start practically from scratch every time—at least, so it feels to me. But as soon as I try once again, and I awaken, I can see that it all gathers up: the awakening of awareness *is* cumulative!

It can be easy and it is. It gets better and better. Sweeter. Juicier. Creativier.

The whole point of awakening is for *you*—the human being and person—to step into your complete power right here and now, and undertake your destined purpose in the vast mosaic of this marvelous adventure we call life!

Whatever your passion and talents are—and I am certain we all have them! —you will discover them for real when you truly awaken, and instead of wasting your time and waning away, you'll get creative and conductive and super productive. In your area of creation, you'll excel beyond your wildest dreams, and even if you never become famous or recognized, *you* will know that you are doing your part and bringing in your piece of the puzzle for everybody! And that is what matters—that is your whole life's purpose, isn't it? Well, you tell me...

All I'm saying is that until we experience awakening, all of this is only a dream. Reality commences when we become truly aware of it. That's when we are really born for the first time here in this life as well.

Maybe it's not for everyone, but hopefully, chances are, since you are right here, reading this book together with me and many many others, that you want this.

You are ready. Are you willing to do your work? It will be easy. If it doesn't feel easy—then maybe some miscreative forces are at work here to curb your enthusiasm. Know that the miscreation is a parasite by nature and will do everything it can to control you and keep you sedated, asleep, and docile—to forever keep using you and your extreme outbursts of energy as its food... You knew this, right?

Shall we return to the explanation of what soul syntax is and how it connects to awareness?

Maybe we can take a deep breath together before we continue.

...

This discussion will pacify the mind and ground our passion so it can remain stable and sustainable.

You know, this whole book has been written in soul syntax.

All along, we've been training together in the use of soul syntax, not only in our discussions and explorations, but also in conversations that each of us has had internally, in our respective heads. Yes, our internal dialog can adopt soul syntax, which is a grand step on the avenue to outcreating the miscreation!

When I say syntax, that doesn't refer just to language or linear processes, like thinking or understanding. No, it encompasses practically everything you can think of and imagine, everything you can sense and experience, do or not do.

Essentially, opening up to the soul syntax means that we are allowing the flow of awareness to ebb between us and Spirit as freely as we can. We're letting go of rigid expectations and shiny goals: we're just here for the joy ride! For the experience of walking the path of awakening.

Oh, what joy, what fun, to get rid of this super-seriousness we're stuck with in our lives!

What freedom lies beyond, if we only dare to go there!

Yet, like everything, it is circular: wanting and trying to do that too much, again becomes a super-serious task in and of itself...

So what to do?

The shamans of ancient Mexico to the rescue once again! Joking aside, there is an extraordinary concept in Castaneda's books which is unique for our modern age: it's called the *not doing*.

At the risk of doing injustice to the original description of it, I'll paraphrase what *not doing* is, in the context of this book. And see, this already is *not doing*: to discuss a key notion, which should demand the most serious argumentation and almost solemn presentation, in a light, near-joking manner.

Why would I do that? Is that disrespect or sheer stupidity? Who knows...

What I believe, as a primal explorer, is that our only chance of sailing safely between the Scylla and Charybdis of the many extremes in our dual, polar, mind-based reality, is to approach jovially even the most dead-serious matters, yet still express due respect by *exchanging* with this world.

I'm mixing sources, references, and metaphors freely as I go, again, not because nothing matters, but because everything does. Because we want to confuse the brain to a certain degree, while still making friends with the mind—it is a part of our whole, after all.

And *not doing* is just that: we play along and take the mind both seriously yet not-seriously, easily allowing all that it wants and yearns for, letting it have all of its tricks and little quirks, and we sincerely love it for its intelligence. The practice of breathwork can teach you this, in a soft way.

One of the main functions of the mind is to keep track of stuff, to itemize lists of just about everything in your life. Instead of running away or fighting against that—realizing that such resistance is quite the opposite of awakening awareness—we still willingly go along with it. We let the mind linearly understand and explain the Universe—that is the *doing*—but whatever the end result of that process, we choose to not linger on it too much, or at all. That's the *not doing* part. We do the heavy work of thinking and understanding and even doing—in any normal, everyday situation and for any task at hand, just as if we truly believe it matters, and yet we know it does *and* doesn't. And we're perfectly aware of that. We don't rely on the mind alone. We have faith.

To a degree, all of the tools for awakening awareness described and mentioned in this book, are *not doing*.

How does the mind understand our tinkering with intuition, dreaming, and awareness? How does the mind look at us as we ascribe all that importance to awakening and the Spirit and what not? Well, the mind gets confused. It wants to bring some order back to the chaos of it. It wants to explain away the unknown and unknowable.

When we engage in *not doing,* we let it do its thing, gracefully and gratefully.

We toy with our beliefs and convictions to the point that the whole old story we have been telling ourselves for our entire life starts to seem a bit boring.

We open up the space of possibilities. We care less for what is true and what is not. Our grip has been softened. This is *not doing*.

Not doing as words or writing may be poetry. Other great examples are the Zen koans: so incomprehensible, mysterious, and sometimes downright crazily nonsensical—and yet they are doorways to awakening awareness! My own collection of self-love koans has been something I've been exchanging with for years as a process of awakening myself into the soul syntax. Those can be found in my *Ink by Star* book series...

Not doing is a bridge over the paradox of taking something extremely seriously and not giving a damn at the same time. Grounded in the awakened awareness, *not doing* is not just an arbitrary, whimsical act, but a key aspect of soul syntax.

Another key aspect of soul syntax is a conscious discernment between the mind and awareness. Living in a society that uses the words "mind" and "awareness" or "consciousness" practically interchangeably, this is important to stress, or de-stress. *Not stress.*

We have said that soul syntax is not a set of rules, but now we can add that it's more an infinite stream of *not rules*, which we make up as we go, relying on our intuition as primal explorers.

These last chapters especially belong even more to the soul syntax and are as such perhaps harder, if not impossible, to understand with the linear mind. Soul syntax implies trust and faith beyond the safety of the known understanding. Many of the paragraphs and segments in this book serve mainly to calm down the mind, and have no other significance in terms of bringing in useful information or knowledge. When it comes to awakening awareness, knowledge is just not as helpful as someone might believe.

If you find it relaxing, here are some more of my intuitions about the new soul syntax.

Soul syntax means that when you discuss something, you don't rely on just knowledge or facts, which of course are merely beliefs. You discuss things as a primal explorer, also inviting everybody else involved to be a primal explorer. On top of that, you don't rely on the mind alone. You create ways of awakening awareness even without understanding what that means or how it is done. You open your heart as best you can; you feel the flow; you sense everything around you and within you. Then you tune up your intuition, your subtle grokking of everything, and open yourself up to whatever comes to you. You gratefully hold space for everyone else to contribute their own insights and then together, you find ways of integrating it all. So again, soul syntax is not a set of rules, but more of a vibration of how we *do* and how we *can* do things—not just talking and thinking about them, but also doing them.

Soul syntax is about knowing that you have something to learn from everybody that you meet. You intuitively see their wounds. You see where they are in their life. Even when they hurt you, you understand why. Lastly, you see whether they see you back or whether they are willing to try. You see whether they know that you are in their life for a reason as well.

Sometimes I call this new syntax, *sacred syntax,* or even *soul syntax science*. However, it is not really anything new, but more like doing away with most, if not all, of the old. As primal explorers, we can learn to leave meanings undefined or at least fluid, ever-shifting, and perennially bobbing up and down in the flow of creation. The new syntax is your willingness to pause, suspend all your judgment, and give the benefit of the doubt to absolutely every idea that comes into your presence, whatever its source. Even if you disagree with it or fear, abhor, or judge it. Especially then: you approach it very attentively and soberly.

The old syntax is and has always been about everybody adhering to it. True, it was helpful in the sense of bridging the gaps between our differences, as a common set of rules and models that we all seemed to adopt. The problem with the old syntax is that it is not nearly powerful enough to encompass the totality of a human existence, including awareness and Spirit. So when we all think our viewpoints and individual experiences are being successfully communicated amongst ourselves through the syntax, that is never true. We believe that nothing is lost in translation, because we trust the syntax—because we ultimately trust the mind, blindly. Our whole society is built on trusting the mind alone. That's why the miscreation can use the submind to control every aspect of our lives, unless we awaken our awareness.

The new soul syntax is not as much a definition of anything as it is an *invitation* to an agreement on a conscious perceptual level, common to the whole of humanity. The new syntax redefines the very meaning and role of a syntax. It's not about linear rules or viewpoints to see, follow, or understand. Instead, it's about the ongoing current of the ever-awakening awareness of everything we choose to focus on. It is infinitely flexible, completely free, and totally empowering.

The shift of human awareness, which precedes or comes with soul syntax, starts with a collective shift of the prevalent viewpoint. It goes beyond mere understanding or learning something new. It's almost an act of creation on a universal level—something we can only do together, as a species. Our co-creation will enable us to perceive and experience a common expanded reality. What is now only a dream, imagination, or intuition of things to come, will blossom into a fully-blown, all-inclusive, absolute and objective reality, which will become the normal, standard foundation of the common cognition we will all share.

We have no idea yet what is truly coming. It's impossible to grasp how and how much we will develop and grow. New vistas will open up as we approach and traverse the landscape of humanity's fate.

This all begins with a plain choice that each and every one of us is bound to make, sooner or later: the choice to sincerely and ultimately awaken to who we are. Yes, this awakening also includes all the answers, information, and guidelines to the whole process—the process called life. It will all come together the moment we start telling ourselves the new story, one of empowerment, fulfillment, and the pure joy of existence. No more need to play small and wait for the world to act first.

It's *your* turn now.

It's time.

Sure, the mind demands a clear understanding of everything. Whatever is not clear is taken as a threat to the mind's supreme control, and it will be either destroyed or denied. Yet here we are in the Universe of pure mystery where nothing is linear or digital in nature. Of course, the mind will immediately deny this and present proof to the contrary. But since it is all circular, who can we ultimately trust? That is the choice we're making moment to moment and with it we're creating a compass of our purpose.

If we choose to trust awareness and intuition, we still need to train ourselves to be able to function in this world without the interference and assistance of the customary mind's control—which will definitely prove to be no easy task. Of course, nothing reasonably specific can be told about that experience, as it is currently outside the reach of our understanding.

Soul syntax is not *yet another* mind-based system designed to offer an illusion of transcending the mind's control. We've had many "new" syntaxes like that. This one is like nothing anyone would expect. And yes, I'm making it all up as I go. Nevertheless, *in the new syntax*, I'd actually use different words for that: I have faith and I'm following my innermost intuition regarding what is truly important about humanity's next step. I'm translating this to linear words as best as I can.

My intuition says the less we focus on any kind of paradigm or system, the freer we are to expand naturally. The new syntax is all but syntax then. It's a non-syntax, but placed on top of our present rules of engagement with life. It's the letting go of syntax. It's about integrating the paradoxes. It's about following the spirit of everything, not the letter. Going directly to the essence of it all.

As I said: this whole book has already been putting the new syntax into practice right from the start.

The new syntax is all about awareness. It's not about the actual content of the message, but its essence, taking into account the flow of everything involved as much as possible, starting by undefining the "I" in the narrative.

My friend and teacher David Elliott uses the new syntax—among everything else he does and shares—for his definition of *exchange*, which starts with "Exchange is a flow of consciousness..."

Using the new syntax is another way of saying that the reporter/writer and the audience/reader are both opening up to their intuitive sides with full awareness, while creating a bridge of communication. Neither of them are building on top of old facts, which are merely current beliefs and convictions.

We—you, dear reader, and I—can witness this in practice here and now. In the new syntax, all matters are equally important and equally difficult or simple to convey.

In fact, none of it even matters any longer!

Or using the new syntax, should we even say "in fact"?

Why yes, that's the whole beauty and novelty of the new syntax: no rules. There are no mind-based formulas to rigidly follow, while we can still freely use anything of the old syntax we want. We trust that the communication channel will just work. It's never been about bringing the information across, like it is with digital computers. Rather, it becomes more about trust and honesty, which are created by choice as we go.

If there are still any rules to follow, they will be like river banks. They give direction and purpose to the river, and lend it support, but only temporarily—as rivers may change their trajectories, and so shall we humans, in the new syntax.

The shamans of ancient Mexico determined that for as long as human beings are born with the mind, there is really no avoiding linear thought, dualism, and rules. But through many generations of shamanistic practice, they have also demonstrated that it isn't necessary to take the mind seriously! Yes, we can use it, follow it for a little while, play along, even believe its digital constructs—and then we can simply throw it all away, being fully aware of its true nature and role in our lives. That's the *not doing* we talked about before.

Our beliefs are not meant to be rigid, permanent, or sacred. The mind is a tool that can be much more useful if we do not consider it a god. As far as I can tell, the only way of grasping this and truly putting it into practice, is to awaken from it first: to awaken awareness! All else is unreal, like a dream within a dream...

Another aspect of soul syntax is creation. We create our perception, its interpretation, and our emotional responses to it, right down to our overall mood. We can choose our mood and we can choose our viewpoints. We create how we feel about anything. It is within our ability to open up to this innate magical power and start living a more volitional life. If we want to save the world or make it a better place, we can start by choosing to feel better about it in the first place. We can choose to feel better about ourselves—which can be one way of learning self-love.

Then we ground that feeling and make it real.

Grounding is a way to feel what *resonates* with you as the truth, or *a* truth: the true reality, for you at this moment. As we ground, we don't even need all that much explaining and understanding—we just *know*. That's the intuition, the claircognizance, or some other *clair-way*.

You see, I don't have to tell you what soul syntax is. You already know. We all do. We may not all be in sync on the rational level, but our innermost connection with all that is, with an awareness-based eternal field, is something we are perennially soaked in. We are permeated with it. We are ceaselessly connected.

Choosing to use the new syntax, whatever that means to you, is another helpful tool for awakening our awareness. Open your heart and your inner eyes—and I's—and consciously continue creating the sense and purpose of your life.

When we reach an unwritten, unexpressed, and even un-understood agreement for using the new syntax, the many issues of communication in all of our relationships will melt away. Each of us will outcreate those perceived, old problems by focusing on something real instead. I just love the word *outcreate*! Do you already know what it means?

By outcreating the miscreation and applying the new syntax to everything internally, we don't have to really destroy anything to move on. There is no need for something to be wrong before something else becomes right or true. Remember, truth is merely a mind-based construct, easy to outcreate. All the talk of shifting into a new paradigm, the old system collapsing, or having to break away from the demons or the evil—all that can be outcreated in the new syntax. The whole of the old syntax can be outcreated in the new syntax.

There is no old and new syntax. There's only awareness and our choice of creation. Ultimately, we want to intend or dream forward our life and dream forward the whole world. As you become aware of this power of creation, you are outcreating through time—and we may call this the new syntax. No need to know what it is or to understand it. We just use it.

Once more, just between you and me: what do we want? Where are we going with this?

My only choice here is to bring more awareness in. I want to outcreate the mind-based interpretations of the world, vanquish the submind, and open everything into the infinite potentiality that is our pre-birth right.

Honestly, I don't yet completely *know* what I want, or who I am.

I'm intuiting—just now—that the Universe is perfect as it is and needs no resolving. There is even a place for the suffering and lack of awareness—there is a place for everything.

I don't know why I am here.

What I do know, is that beyond the confines of the mind awaits a whole other reality—the true home of soul syntax.

That is where I'm headed.

This is why I *want* to be here. This is what I *am* here for.

What about you?

"Agreement is overrated."
—Ink by Star, Book 22: *Ursa Minor*

Conclusion

The conclusion, in all honesty, is here to offer the mind one last argument and reason for taking this book and these words seriously enough to give them a fair chance, and to inspire experimentation with the tools of awakening described herein. Just like all along, I will carefully enfold the sting of the mind's critical control into a soft wrap of safe elucidation, a plausible conclusion, a quiet lull, so the mind will at least become curious, if not yet convinced.

What would make you believe that this *is* important? Could you believe that awakening awareness is something we all should pursue and practice daily, beginning in primary school?

Put in other words: you reading this, tells me, through time and space, that at least a part of you is interested. Perhaps you have been looking for explanations or answers to certain *fateful* experiences. Or maybe you feel alone—perhaps you are different from the "norm" and being here brings you some peace and hope that, well, you are not the only one—not the only dreamer out there...

I can only say that this—awakening awareness—is what I believe and how I live.

Writing this book and others like it is, in my opinion, the best contribution I can ever make to helping other beings on this blue planet—by inspiring at least some of you to open up to your innermost secrets and powers—of love and awareness.

I want to stress how vital, I believe, awakening is for you, me, and all of humanity. I want to highlight how crucial it is that we learn the all-important, essential distinction between the mind and that which we call awareness—and to accept that we can only ever grok the difference experientially, on the level of awareness, not using the mind alone—which is again circular, and therefore demands a leap of faith. This is easiest done by a consistent, dedicated, regular practice. You don't have to really know what awareness is, to awaken from the slumber of diminished awareness that infects our everyday, routine, pre-programmed life.

On top of it all, our traumas and powerful negative past experiences, sometimes inherited through generations, can—and normally do—cause us to disassociate from reality, and we become ungrounded from Mother Nature and our own self-love—our very birthright. Ironically, to protect ourselves from exactly that which we are eagerly rushing towards, we fall prey to a devious voice coming from what I call the submind, and we set out to create, out of nothing, a miscreation. This miscreation becomes a separate field of energy, living within our energetic being, that feeds off our extreme emotions like the true parasite that it is. In order to remain in charge and keep its constant control over everything we perceive, believe, and choose, the miscreation via the submind leads us to follow anything we think would make us loved and safe, but we end up being served just the opposite. That's how the miscreation works: through devious deception, which makes us *feel abuse as love*—believe it or not.

The way through this terrible predicament—perhaps the only way—is to awaken from the illusion. But our cage and our escaping it is not something as linear and logical as, for example, a constructed matrix placed over our reality from which you can simply be unplugged, like from an electrical outlet. Nor is it something practically fantastic like waking up from a terrifying nightmare using a magical spell or a secret formula. No. None of this deus-ex-machina hollywood hocus pocus will ever work in reality.

First, we have to sincerely want to sober up, do our homework, and learn the ropes of what binds us on the levels that nobody has told us anything about. Forget all that you know. All the spiritual books you have devoured and the retreats you've been to—let them go. Even though knowledge has value and it is being brought forward by wise and trustworthy messengers—the question is: is your sacred vessel clear enough to receive that nectar? What if you can only ever drink of pure waters that are sourced out of your own depths, and have been cleansed and energized through your own divine experience? At least temporarily, release absolutely everything and become a true primal explorer. Start from Scratch. Use nothing else but pure intuition, fly on fumes of faith, and stop at nothing—keep your focus fluid and forever flowing.

But enough of all alliteration. Suffice it to say that there are no rules, and this is the good news: as you honestly decide to embark on this exploration and set up your innermost intent, know that whichever ideology floats your boat, will do. Meaning: whatever you are doing, whichever tools and practices you are using—if you put your whole heart to it, you will succeed: you *will* awaken! In that respect, you can't go wrong. So take my advice and don't even worry about it. Don't overthink it. Just do it. Yes, I said that. Why not?

Have faith that you are *not alone*. That said, you don't need any support system or external help. Trust your intuitive guidance—or just make it up! As soon as you are sovereign enough to dare quieting the mind and opening your heart, all else will follow. You'll know your next step when you take this first one. And when you awaken to your soul's awareness, you'll know who you truly are and what you are here for: your sacred purpose. Or, again, you'll make one up. That counts too, because you're the captain of your soul.

Let me summarize and share four simple intuitions for you to savor if you would.

1. Awareness is your truth and power. You will know who you

are and what you want in your life—your purpose.

2. Take action and seize your day. Immerse yourself in every moment, even the hurt and sorrow. Let go of all control and rise in your faith and you will feel at peace and worthy.

3. Sense the unity of all existence firsthand. No need to argue. Be the love instead of being right. Exchange in a balanced way, full of sweetness.

4. Trust your intuition. Use the mind as a tool for rational processing; don't let it use you and tell you what to do to accomplish results that are disconnected from Mother Nature.

In my vision, humanity is the latest step of the Universe's evolution. This movement is a new foray into an unprecedented territory: the realm of the digital, logical, and dual. The mind is a new quality of existence. On one side, it offers all human beings a stronger concentration of experience and a higher density of realness. But on the other hand, the mind unfortunately makes our beliefs infinitely rigid. We are now able to spin illusion on top of solid reality, and submerge ourselves in it so completely that we get lost.

We are presently at the lowest point of this grand turn of the spiral. The revolution of the mind has severed us from the Nature of Mother Earth and we are living a nightmare without really knowing why. The mind's illusion on the top of reality directs our focus on self-perpetuated strife and alienation, separation from each other and the whole, and confusion, doubts, and fears. We want to annihilate this negativity by yearning for positivity, but all we do is constantly oscillate between the two, never awakening beyond the totalitarian control of the mind.

In other words, what the mind projects into our awareness appears nightmarish to us, and we want to fix that. We struggle and fight each other to kill the monster, whereas in truth our problem is not the projections, but the projector—the way we let it work.

My deepest intuition is that we are already emerging from the mists of illusion into the bright lights of transmutation, moving towards the integration of the dual mind into a singular, quantum-enlightened *supermind*. I borrow the term supermind from Sri Aurobindo, an Indian mystic from the previous century, who wrote about this evolution extensively.

The birth of the supermind will be painful, I feel, but only as much as we find it hard to let go of linear control and abandon ourselves to faith. Having to go against all that we believe is incredibly difficult, but not impossible—because of our magical nature.

As we allow our soul and Spirit to guide us—through our intuition—into the depths of our hearts, where the vibration of our self-love is generated and from where it spreads to every cell and fiber of our body, we imbue our energy being with consciousness, and this completely transforms us into what we are as the next quantum leap on our evolutionary path.

And even the mind—the seat of ego, separation, dualism, and consequently all negativity, aggression, self-denigration and self-destruction—is transmuting to the supermind. The mind, however, will never be able to recognize or know its offspring, the supermind, and will ironically fear it and perhaps try to suffocate it in its cradle.

That inner strife is what we experience as suffering.

Only awakened awareness and self-love can transcend and then transmute the pain of this endless, pointless self-fight. But first we have to become clearly aware of the fact that we are not fighting demons, evil, or darkness—we are actually attacking ourselves: one part of our own being is waging merciless war against another part.

As within, so without.

This is not a schism between the brothers and sisters of humanity—instead, we are primarily polarized and split within, cracked to our core, with even our powers of cognition broken to the point where we can't possibly detect our only true fault. Our fault is that in order to save ourselves, we attempt to deal with the projections of the mind, instead of turning the projector off entirely.

Still, as we keep meditating daily, letting Spirit flow into our being, and outcreating the mind's control, our consciousness will be re-awakening time and again, until the mind will ultimately be transmuted to the supermind—something we can't yet imagine. In this process, the new syntax will emerge on its own and the infinite mysteries of the Universe and Spirit will finally be revealed to a human being, not only through intuition, but with divine understanding as well.

Do the work.

It can be easy. Whenever it's not—mind you—it's probably just the illusion getting the better of you.

Good. End of the sweet wrapper. A bone for the mind to chew on, but in a good way, for sure. We need all of it, the white and the black, for as long as we play the game of duality.

Let me conclude now and say farewell to you with what I wrote down in my notes as a possible alternative introduction, if I dared to lead with it.

"The art of a healer is to deliver the message under the impossible conditions."

—Ink by Star, Book 22: *Ursa Minor*

Speak to me plainly

I wish I could simply say that these are the steps to follow:
1. We are all trapped in the mind.

2. The only way through is awareness.

3. Nobody knows what awareness really is.

4. We cannot be told what awareness is.

5. The only way to understand awareness is to practice its awakening.

6. If you ever want to know what awareness is, you have to change.

7. You have to do the work.

8. I can't reach you, but you can reach me.

Imagine that we are trapped within a dream. How would you ever tell that to others so they could believe you? I've been trying to do this for decades. It never worked. Now I know I have to use a different syntax, a new syntax. But this new syntax is not really a syntax. It's a way of using the same syntax from a different angle. It all begins with that old question: who are you? The new syntax takes this question into account.

The only way you can hear what I'm telling you is for you to awaken. And to awaken, you need to practice daily. You need to meditate daily. By *meditate*, I mean to learn to pause your thoughts, the mind. After years of practice, the mind *will* go quiet. Only then you will realize the mind has been hijacked, but not necessarily by an evil entity. The way I see it, we hijack the mind ourselves: with our routines of following patterns that go against our greater good. These patterns might be inherited family beliefs, social programs, or denial and resistance as a consequence of personal trauma.

There *is* a way through this!

But you need to do the work. You need to practice awakening daily. Then your awareness *will* shift and you will *know*.

Do you want to know how?

Read on.

The problem for many of us, is that we get stuck in purgatory. When trying to awaken, we stumble and mistake a virtual awareness, a mere construct of the mind, for the real thing, and then spend years believing how spiritual we are, and that we are awakening, whereas in fact, we simply pretend to chase our tails.

How will you know what true awareness is?

Read on...

Breathwork Meditation Recording

This 14-minute breathwork meditation recording has been created for you as a sacred offering to accompany *Soul Syntax*.

You can freely access and download it at this link:

ss14.breathwork.fun

Have fun with it and may it support you on your path, wherever you go!

Healing Tools

Subscribe to my newsletter on **www.borutlesjak.com** to keep in touch and be advised of the forthcoming sequels and other healing materials—get your **FREE Borut Lesjak's healing quick start kit**, including the **complete *Breathwork Healing* e-book**, the **7-minute *One Moon Present* breathwork meditation**, and the ***One Moon Present* formula's beautifully designed set of cheat

sheets. You will also receive invitations to **advanced-reader copies** of my new books, and an occasional, never-before published chapter from both behind the scenes and from the great beyond.

Visit **www.borutlesjak.com** to get to know me better, follow my blog, and for a wide selection of breathwork meditations and a variety of self-help, awakening, self-love, and children's books to choose from.

About the Author

Borut Lesjak is an intuitive healer and author from Slovenia. Since childhood, he has been drawn to grok the mystery of existence. During the vulnerable years of his carefree youth, he awakened to the awareness of death and life, discovering a gift of claircognizance. Life hard-rocked the sensitive adult Lesjak to a state of hopeless haze until he ignited an inner choice to heal himself. Breathwork meditation coupled with creative expression opened his heart and mind to restore his innocence. Grounded by realness larger than life, he found his calling by bringing clarity, compassion, integration, and joy to this beloved planet for all to experience.

After residing and working in Australia, USA, Mexico, and Paris, France, he is now stationed in magical Geneva, Switzerland, where he lives with his wife and three children and works a grounding job as a tech consultant, while writing books and offering awareness-awakening and healing sessions. He loves to dream, drive, travel, jog, and hike. He is having fun.

You can connect with Borut at **www.borutlesjak.com** or stalk him on social media. He self-publishes, and personally reads and promptly responds to his email at **borut@borutlesjak.com**.

"Borut Lesjak is a force of nature, and his unflinching, radical commitment to healing, growth and the transformative power of love is brought to life in The Snowflake, a gentle tale about the journey towards union and the magic of harmony with the wild world."

—Sarah Berti, mythmaker, author of The Helix Library Mythos

Also By

Soul Awareness Awakening series
Soul Syntax
Soul Science
Soul Society

Self-Love Healing series
Breathwork Healing
The Healing Power of Self-Love
Self-Love Healing Quick Reference

Love Yourself Through series
Love Yourself Through Fear
Love Yourself Through Anger
Love Yourself Through Sadness

Breathwork Healing Meditations series
Soul Syntax Breathwork Meditation
One Moon Present Breathwork Meditation
Love Yourself Through Fear Breathwork Meditation
Love Yourself Through Anger Breathwork Meditation

Love Yourself Through Sadness Breathwork Meditation

Ink by Star series
Orion
Cassiopeia
Andromeda
Cygnus
Lyra
Phoenix
Canis Major
Aries
Taurus
Gemini
Cancer
Leo
Virgo
Libra
Scorpius
Sagittarius
Capricornus
Aquarius
Pisces
Ophiuchus
Pegasus
Ursa Minor
Milky Way

Sen & Sanja series
Sen, Sanja, and the Cube of Runes
Sen, Sanja, and the Clock of Mirrors
Sen, Sanja, and the Coat of Dreams

Mother Earth series
The Snowflake

The Cloud
The Wind
The Sun
The Tree
The River
The Snowman

9 7 9 8 2 2 4 2 5 9 1 2 0